IRON HEART

IRON HEART
SURVIVING TOUGH TIMES

The Prince
by Niccolò Machiavelli

The Art of War
by Sun Tzu

Power and Wealth
by Ralph Waldo Emerson

Atom-Smashing Power of Mind
by Charles Fillmore

*The Million-Dollar Secret
Hidden In Your Mind*
by Anthony Norvell

abridged and introduced by
Mitch Horowitz

MEDIA

Published 2020 by Gildan Media LLC
aka G&D Media.
www.GandDmedia.com

Cover design by David Rheinhardt of Pyrographx

Interior design by Meghan Day Healey of Story Horse, LLC.

ISBN: 978-1-7225-0517-2

CONTENTS

PREFACE

The Meaning of Strength

What is mental toughness? In earlier eras, that question was easily (often too easily) responded to. In Victorian times, it meant not complaining in the face of adversity. An admirable goal—but one that frequently spilled over into impersonal falseness and emotional distance.

I am not sure that things are much better today, when we are taught to use therapeutic or spiritual language but sometimes deploy it to evade responsibility. I realized that this aspect of our culture had gone overboard when a negligent institutional debtor asked me to show "compassion" for its accounting department. On the opposite polarity, the language of sarcasm and overt hate abound online.

So, again, what is a healthy model of mental and emotional resiliency, traits that are urgently needed during this period of virus-driven lockdown and ruinous recession? I think the works abridged in this collection point us in the right direction. Cumulatively, these writings, each of which features its own introduction, teach personal agency, ethics, strategy, and persistence. Their central principle is meaningful fortitude.

The title *Iron Heart* may seem histrionic, especially by today's standards. But look again. I was inspired by a story I personally heard about the residency director of a surgical program. The director told his charges: "After this residency, you will have the heart of a lion and the touch of a lamb." That ethic is at the back of this collection.

You may be surprised at some of the books condensed in this anthology. Good. Our purpose is to look anew at authors who are not fully understood. Nourishing ideas are often neglected. A case in point is *The Prince* by Niccolò Machiavelli, the supposedly ruthless promoter of amoral power grabbing. But the rules of survival found in *The Prince* train you to deal with a world that is itself amoral and to engage it in a way that doesn't deepen but navigates the morass.

The ancient work of martial philosophy *The Art of War* is another textured approach to a threatening world. The master Sun Tzu's chief lessons are three: 1) The greatest solider never fights—his evident strength makes it unnecessary. 2) When a fight is unavoidable, adopt the nature of water: be ever-changing, dwell unseen at the depths, and strike with irresistible force. 3) After victory is won return quickly to peace. Standing armies whither in the field.

Ralph Waldo Emerson's classic essays *Power and Wealth* demonstrate, with admirable practicality, how to enact the

Transcendentalist's principles of self-reliance in daily life. The key to power, Emerson writes, is focusing on a single aim or source of excellence, and repeatedly working at it to the exclusion of all secondary concerns. The rule to wealth is spending your money in ways that facilitate earning more of it.

I believe that our ideals and mental images do more than shape our psychology and ethics but they have an outpicturing effect on our world. Charles Fillmore's *Atom-Smashing Power of Mind* was the Unity founder's attempt to show that we are only as great as our ability to control and manage the technologies we have mentally birthed. When power exceeds ethics, power destroys.

This collection is capped by Anthony Norvell's *The Million-Dollar Secret Hidden in Your Mind*. I have a deep affection for this guide to success because it endorses all of the maneuvering and hustling that is necessary in life but teaches doing so with honor, dignity, and reciprocity—traits that you can never possess enduring strength without.

As we struggle to arrive at and decipher how the world will look following the pandemic, it is clear that we need individuals who pull wagons rather than just ride in them, broadly defined. The works collected in *Iron Heart* teach you how to be that indispensable person.

—Mitch Horowitz

THE PRINCE

THE PRINCE

*History's Greatest Guide
to Attaining and Keeping Power—
Now In a Special Condensation*

Niccolò Machiavelli

THE CONDENSED 📖 CLASSICS LIBRARY™

Contents

Introduction

A Different Side of The Prince

by Mitch Horowitz

It does not come naturally to me to introduce and abridge Niccolò Machiavelli's 1532 classic *The Prince*. The Renaissance-era guide to gaining and holding power has been known for centuries as a blueprint to ruthlessness, deception, and even brutality. I have inveighed against current books, like *The 48 Laws of Power*, that endorse amoral or unethical methods of personal advancement.

"But that's the real world," argue the defenders of such books. Not my world. And not the one I encourage others to dwell in.

How, then, do I justify this condensed and reader-friendly new edition of *The Prince*, a book considered the urtext of guides to ruthless attainment? The fact is—as you will discover in this careful abridgement—the writer and diplomat Machiavelli imbued his work with a greater sense of purpose and ethics than is commonly understood. Although Machiavelli unquestionably endorses absolutist and, at times, bloody ways of dealing with adversaries, he repeatedly notes that these are efforts of a last or near-last resort, when peaceable means of governance prove either unpromising or unworkable. He justifies resorting to deception or faithlessness only as a defense against the depravity of men, who shift alliances like the winds. This logic by no means approaches the morality of Christ's principle to be "wise as serpents and harmless as doves," but it belies the general notion that Machiavelli was a one-dimensional schemer.

Moreover, the author also emphasizes rewarding merit; leaving the public to its own devices and personal pursuits as much as possible (which is the essential ingredient to developing culture and economy); trusting subjects enough to allow them to bear arms—and even to arm them yourself if confident in their loyalty (which the good leader should be); surrounding oneself with wise counselors (the true measure of an able ruler); avoiding and not exploiting civic divisions; and striving to ensure the public's general satisfaction.

One of the most striking parts of the book for me is when Machiavelli expounds on the best kind of intellect for an adviser or minister. In chapter XVII he writes:

> *There are three scales of intelligence, one which under-*
> *stands by itself, a second which understands what it*

is shown by others, and a third, which understands neither by itself nor by the showing of others, the first of which is most excellent, the second good, but the third worthless.

This has always been my favorite passage of Machiavelli's. To add a further dimension to his observation, here is an alternate translation (and I challenge you to consider what place you have earned on its scale):

There exist three kinds of intellects: that belonging to the one who can do the thing itself, that belonging to the one who can judge the thing, and that belonging to the one who can neither do nor judge. The first is excellent, the second is good, and the third is worthless.

Some contemporary critics suggest that *The Prince* is actually a satire of monarchy: that under the guise of a guide to ruthless conduct Machiavelli sends up the actions of absolute rulers and covertly calls for more republican forms of government. I think this assessment probably stretches matters. But it would be equally wrong, as noted, to conclude that Machiavelli was a narrow-eyed courtier bent on keeping others down. On balance, Machiavelli was a pragmatic tutor interested in promoting the unity, stability, and integrity of nation states, chiefly his own Italy, in a Europe that lacked cohesive civics and reliable international treaties. His harsher ideas were then considered acceptable quivers in the bow of statecraft; you will also see his efforts to leaven them with keen observations about the vicissitudes of human nature, fate, and virtue.

In actuality, I believe that businesspeople, leaders, and entrepreneurs who read *The Prince* today will discover subtleties that are missing from current power-at-any-cost guides. I advise experiencing *The Prince* through the filter of your own ethical standards and inner truths; sifting among its practical lessons; taking in its tough observations about human weaknesses; and using it as a guide to the realities—and foibles—of how we live.

Let me say a brief word about my method of abridgment. First, I have used the 1910 translation of Renaissance scholar N.H. Thomson, which originally appeared as part of the Harvard Classics line. My aim in condensing Thomson's translation is to provide the full range of Machiavelli's lessons and observations, but without most of his historical portraiture (which is well worth reading in the original, if you are engaged by what you encounter here). I have taken Machiavelli's most relatable and practical passages and ordered them into individual segments, each with a new and clarifying title. I have striven to eliminate repetition. I have occasionally substituted modern terms for antiquated ones. Finally, I have included a closing section of Machiavelli's most poignant aphorisms.

To the Reader

———•·•———

I have found among my possessions none that I prize
and esteem more than a knowledge of the actions of
great men, acquired in the course of long experience
in modern affairs and a continual study of antiquity. This
knowledge has been most carefully and patiently pondered
over and sifted by me, and now reduced into this little
book. I can offer no better gift than the means of master-
ing, in a very brief time, all that in the course of so many
years, and at the cost of so many hardships and dangers, I
have learned, and know.

—Niccolò Machiavelli

CHAPTER I

On Acquiring a New Kingdom

The Prince cannot avoid giving offense to new subjects, either in respect of the troops he quarters on them, or of some other of the numberless vexations attendant on a new acquisition. And in this way you may find that you have enemies in all those whom you have injured in seizing the Princedom, yet cannot keep the friendship of those who helped you to gain it; since you can neither reward them as they expect, nor yet, being under obligations to them, use violent remedies against them. For however strong you may be in respect of your army, it is essential that in entering a new Province you should have the good will of its inhabitants.

Hence it happened that Louis XII of France speedily gained possession of Milan, and as speedily lost it. For the very people who had opened the gates to the French King, when they found themselves deceived in their expectations and hopes of future benefits, could not put up with the insolence of their new ruler.

True it is that when a State rebels and is again got under, it will not afterwards be lost so easily. For the Prince, using the rebellion as a pretext, will not hesitate to secure himself by punishing the guilty, bringing the suspected to trial, and otherwise strengthening his position in the points where it was weak.

I say, then, that those States which upon their acquisition are joined onto the ancient dominions of the Prince who acquires them are either of the same religion and language as the people of these dominions, or they are not. When they are, there is great ease in retaining them, especially when they have not been accustomed to live in freedom. To hold them securely it is enough to have rooted out the line of the reigning Prince; because if in other respects the old condition of things be continued, and there be no discordance in their customs, men live peaceably with one another. Even if there be some slight difference in their languages, provided that customs are similar, they can easily get on together. He, therefore, who acquires such a State, if he mean to keep it, must see to two things: first, that the blood of the ancient line of Princes be destroyed; second, that no change be made in respect of laws or taxes; for in this way the newly acquired State speedily becomes incorporated.

But when States are acquired in a country differing in language, usages, and laws, difficulties multiply, and great good fortune, as well as actions, are needed to overcome them. One of the best and most efficacious methods for dealing with such a State is for the Prince who acquires it to go and dwell there in person, since this will tend to make his tenure more secure and lasting. For when you are on the spot, disorders are detected in their beginnings and remedies can be readily applied; but when you are at a distance, they are not heard of until they have gathered strength and the case is past cure. Moreover, the Province in which you take up your abode is not pillaged by your officers; the people are pleased to have a ready recourse to their Prince; and have all the more reason if they are well disposed, to love, if disaffected, to fear him. A foreign enemy desiring to attack that State would be cautious how he did so. In short, where the Prince resides in person, it will be extremely difficult to oust him.

Another excellent expedient is to send colonies into one or two places, so that these may become, as it were, the keys of the Province; for you must either do this, or else keep up a numerous force of men-at-arms and foot soldiers. A Prince need not spend much on colonies. He can send them out and support them at little or no charge to himself, and the only persons to whom he gives offence are those whom he deprives of their fields and houses to bestow them on the new inhabitants. Those who are thus injured form but a small part of the community, and remaining scattered and poor can never become dangerous. All others being left unmolested, are in consequence easily quieted, and at the same time are afraid to make a false move, lest they share the fate of those who have been deprived of their possessions. In few words, these colonies cost less than soldiers, are more faithful, and give less offense, while those who are offended, being, as

I have said, poor and dispersed, cannot hurt. And let it here be noted that men are either to be kindly treated, or utterly crushed, since they can revenge lighter injuries, but not graver. Wherefore the injury we do to a man should be of a sort to leave no fear of reprisals.

Chapter II

Against Occupation

I f instead of colonies you send troops, the cost is vastly greater, and the whole revenues of the country are spent in guarding it; so that the gain becomes a loss, and much deeper offense is given; since in shifting the quarters of your soldiers from place to place the whole country suffers hardship, which as all feel, all are made enemies; and enemies who remaining, although vanquished, in their own homes, have power to hurt. In every way, therefore, this mode of defense is as disadvantageous as that by colonizing is useful.

In dealing with the countries of which they took possession the Romans diligently followed the methods I have described. They planted colonies, conciliated weaker powers without adding to their strength, humbled the great, and never suffered a formidable stranger to acquire influence.

CHAPTER III

The Example of Alexander the Great

A lexander the Great having achieved the conquest of Asia in a few years and, dying before he had well entered on possession, it might have been expected, given the difficulty of preserving newly acquired States, that on his death the whole country would rise in revolt.

Nevertheless, his successors were able to keep their hold, and found in doing so no other difficulty than arose from their own ambition and mutual jealousies.

If anyone think this strange and ask the cause, I answer that all the Princedoms of which we have record have been governed in one of two ways: 1) either by a sole Prince, all others being his servants permitted by his grace and favor to assist in governing the kingdom as his ministers; or 2) by a Prince with his Barons who hold their rank, not by the favor of a superior Lord, but by antiquity of bloodline, and who have States and subjects of their own who recognize them as their rulers and entertain for them a natural affection.

States governed by a sole Prince and by his servants— as with Alexander—vest in him a more complete authority;

because throughout the land none but he is recognized as sovereign, and if obedience be yielded to any others, it is yielded as to his ministers and officers for whom personally no special love is felt.*

---

* Machiavelli is saying that civic and military authority surpasses bloodline.—MH

CHAPTER IV

How to Control Formerly Independent Territories

When a newly acquired State has been accustomed to live under its own laws and in freedom, there are three methods whereby it may be held. The first is to destroy it; the second, to go and reside there in person; the third, to suffer it to live on under its own laws, subjecting it to a tribute and entrusting its government to a few of the inhabitants who will keep the rest your friends. Such a Government, since it is the creature of the new Prince, will see that it cannot stand without his protection and support, and must therefore do all it can to maintain him; and a city accustomed to live in freedom, if it is to be preserved at all, is more easily controlled through its own citizens than in any other way.

We have examples of all these methods in the histories of the Spartans and the Romans. The Spartans held Athens and Thebes by creating oligarchies in these cities, yet lost them in the end. The Romans, to retain Capua, Carthage, and Numantia, destroyed them and never lost them. On the other hand, when they thought to hold Greece as the Spartans had held it, leaving it its freedom and allowing it to be governed by its own laws, they failed, and had to destroy many cities of that Province before they could secure it. For, in truth, there is no sure way of holding other than by destroying, and whoever becomes master of a City accustomed to live in freedom and does not destroy it, may reckon on being destroyed by it. For if it should rebel, it can always screen itself under the name of liberty and its ancient laws, which no length of time, nor any benefits conferred will ever cause it to forget; and do what you will, and take what care you may, unless the inhabitants be scattered and dispersed, this name, and the old order of things, will never cease to be remembered, but will at once be turned against you whenever misfortune overtakes you.

If, however, the newly acquired City or Province has been accustomed to live under a Prince, and his line is extinguished, it will be impossible for the citizens, used, on the one hand, to obey, and deprived, on the other, of their old ruler, to agree to choose a leader from among themselves; and as they know not how to live as freemen, and are therefore slow to take up arms, a stranger may readily gain them over and attach them to his cause. But in Republics there is a stronger vitality, a fiercer hatred, a keener thirst for revenge. The memory of their former freedom will not let them rest; so that the safest course is either to destroy them, or to go and live in them.

CHAPTER V

When a Prince
Conquers by Merit

Since men for the most part follow in the footsteps and imitate the actions of others, and yet are unable to adhere exactly to those paths which others have taken, or attain to the virtues of those whom they would resemble, the wise man should always follow the roads that have been trodden by the great, and imitate those who have most excelled, so that if he cannot reach their perfection, he may at least acquire something of its savor. Acting in this like the skillful archer, who seeing that the object he would hit is distant, and knowing the range of his bow, takes aim much above the destined mark; not designing that his arrow should strike so high, but that flying high it may strike the point intended.

I say, then, that in entirely new Princedoms where the Prince himself is new, the difficulty of maintaining possession varies with the greater or less ability of him who acquires possession. And, because the mere fact of a private person rising to be a Prince presupposes either merit or good fortune, it will be seen that the presence of one or other of these two conditions lessens, to some extent, many difficulties. And yet, he who is less beholden to Fortune has often in the end the better success; and it may be for the advantage of a Prince that, from his having no other territories, he is obliged to reside in person in the State which he has acquired.

Looking first to those who have become Princes by their merit and not by their good fortune, I say that the most excellent among them are Moses, Cyrus, Romulus, Theseus, and the like. And though perhaps I ought not to name Moses, he being merely an instrument for carrying out the Divine commands, he is still to be admired for those qualities which made him worthy to converse with God. But if we consider Cyrus and the others who have acquired or founded kingdoms, they will all be seen to be admirable. And if their actions and the particular institutions of which they were the authors be studied, they will be found not to differ from those of Moses, instructed though he was by so great a teacher. Moreover, on examining their lives and actions, we shall see that they were debtors to Fortune for nothing beyond the opportunity which enabled them to shape things as they pleased, without which the force of their spirit would have been spent in vain; as on the other hand, opportunity would have offered itself in vain had the capacity for turning it to account been wanting. It was necessary, therefore, that Moses should find the children of Israel in bondage in Egypt, and oppressed by the Egyptians, in order that they might be disposed to follow him, and so escape from their servitude. It was fortunate for Romulus that he found no home in Alba, but was exposed at the time of his birth, to the end that he might become king and founder of the City of Rome. It was necessary that Cyrus should find the Persians discontented with the rule of the Medes, and the Medes enervated and effeminate from a prolonged peace. Nor could Theseus have displayed his great qualities had he not found the Athenians disunited and dispersed. But while it was their opportunities that made these men fortunate, it was their own merit that enabled them to recognize these opportunities and turn them to account, to the glory and prosperity of their country.

They who come to the Princedom, as these did, by virtuous paths, acquire with difficulty, but keep with ease. The difficulties which they have in acquiring arise mainly from the new laws and institutions that they are forced to introduce in founding and securing their government. And let it be noted that there is no more delicate matter to take in hand, nor more dangerous to conduct, nor more doubtful in its success, than to set up as a leader in the introduction of changes. For he who innovates will have for his enemies all those who are well off under the existing order of things, and only lukewarm supporters in those who might be better off under the new. This lukewarm temper arises partly from the fear of adversaries who have the laws on their side, and partly from the incredulity of mankind, who will never admit the merit of anything new, until they have seen it proved by the event. The result, however, is that whenever the enemies of change make an attack, they do so with all the zeal of partisans, while the others defend themselves so feebly as to endanger both themselves and their cause.

It should be borne in mind that the temper of the multitude is fickle, and that while it is easy to persuade them of a thing, it is hard to fix them in that persuasion. Wherefore, matters should be so ordered that when men no longer believe of their own accord, they may be compelled to believe by force. Moses, Cyrus, Theseus, and Romulus could never have made their ordinances be observed for any length of time had they been unarmed, as was the case, in our own days, with the Friar Girolamo Savonarola, whose new institutions came to nothing so soon as the multitude began to waver in their faith; since he had not the means to keep those who had been believers steadfast in their belief, or to make unbelievers believe.

Such persons, therefore, have great difficulty in carrying out their designs; but all their difficulties are on the road, and may be overcome by courage. Having conquered these, and coming to be held in reverence, and having destroyed all who were jealous of their influence, they remain powerful, safe, honored, and prosperous.

Chapter VI

When a Prince Conquers with Help of Others or by Luck

They who from private life become Princes by mere good fortune, do so with little trouble, but have much trouble to maintain themselves. They meet with no hindrance on their way, being carried as it were on wings to their destination, but all their difficulties overtake them when they alight. Of this class are those on whom States are conferred either in return for money, or through the favor of him who confers them.

Such Princes are wholly dependent on the favor and fortunes of those who have made them great; of supports none could be less stable or secure; and they lack both the knowledge and the power that would enable them to maintain their position. They lack the knowledge because, unless they have great parts and force of character, it is not to be expected that having always lived in a private station they should have learned how to command. They lack the power since they cannot look for support from attached and faithful troops. Moreover, States suddenly acquired, like all else that is produced and grows up rapidly, can never have such root or hold as that the first storm which strikes them shall not overthrow them; unless, indeed that they who suddenly become Princes have a capacity for learning quickly how to defend what Fortune has placed in their lap, and can lay those foundations after they rise which by others are laid before.

He who does not lay his foundations at first, may, if he be of great ability, succeed in laying them afterwards, though with inconvenience to the builder and risk to the building.

A certain type of man will judge it necessary, on entering a new Princedom, to rid himself of enemies, to conciliate friends, to prevail by force or fraud, to make himself feared yet not hated by his subjects, respected and obeyed by his soldiers, to crush those who can or ought to injure him, to introduce changes in the old order of things, to be at once severe and affable, magnanimous and liberal, to do away with a mutinous army and create a new one, to maintain relations with Kings and Princes on such a footing that they must see it for their interest to aid him, and dangerous to offend.

CHAPTER VII

When a Prince Conquers by Crime

A man may also rise from privacy to be a Prince in one of two ways, neither of which can be ascribed wholly either to merit or to fortune. The ways I speak of are, first, when the ascent to power is made by paths of wickedness and crime; and, second, when a private person becomes ruler of his country by the favor of his fellow-citizens.

Whoever examines the first man's actions and achievements will discover little or nothing in them which can be ascribed to Fortune, seeing that it was not through the favor of any but by the regular steps of the military service, gained at the cost of a thousand hardships and hazards, he reached the princedom, which he afterwards maintained by so many daring and dangerous enterprises. Still, to slaughter fellow-citizens, to betray friends, to be devoid of honor, pity, and religion, cannot be counted as merits, for these are means which may lead to power, but which confer no glory.

On seizing a state, the usurper should make haste to inflict what injuries he must, at a stroke, that he may not have to renew them daily, but be enabled by their discontinuance to reassure men's minds and afterwards win them over by benefits. Whosoever, either through timidity or from following bad counsels adopts a contrary course must keep the sword always drawn, and can put no trust in his subjects, who suffering from continued and constantly renewed severities, will never yield him their confidence. Injuries, therefore, should be inflicted all at once that their ill savor being less lasting may the less offend; whereas, benefits should be conferred little by little that so they may be more fully relished.

But, above all things, a Prince should so live with his subjects that no vicissitude of good or evil fortune shall oblige him to alter his behavior; because, if a need to change should come through adversity, it is then too late to resort to severity; while any leniency that you may use will be thrown away, for it will be seen to be compulsory and gain you no thanks.

Chapter VIII

When a Prince Rules by Popular Consent

I come now to the second case, namely, of the leading citizen who, not by crimes or violence, but by the favor of his fellow-citizens is made Prince of his country. This may be called a Civil Princedom, and its attainment depends not wholly on merit, nor wholly on good fortune, but rather on what may be termed a fortunate astuteness. I say then that the road to this Princedom lies either through the favor of the people or of the nobles. For in every city are to be found these two opposed humors having their origin in this: that the people desire not to be domineered over or oppressed by the nobles, while the nobles desire to oppress and domineer over the people. And from these two contrary appetites there arises in cities one of three results: a Princedom, or Liberty, or License. A Princedom is created either by the people or by the nobles, according as one or other of these factions has occasion for it. For when the nobles perceive that they cannot withstand the people, they set to work to magnify the reputation of one of their number, and make him their Prince, to the end that under his shadow they may be enabled to indulge their desires. The people, on the other hand, when they see that they cannot make head against the nobles, invest a single citizen with all their influence and make him Prince, that they may have the shelter of his authority.

He who is made Prince by the favor of the nobles, has greater difficulty to maintain himself than he who comes to the Princedom by aid of the people, since he finds many about him who think themselves as good as he, and whom, on that account, he cannot guide or govern as he would. But he who reaches the Princedom by the popular support, finds himself alone, with none, or but a very few about him who are not ready to obey. Moreover, the demands of the nobles cannot be satisfied with credit to the Prince, nor without injury to others, while those of the people well may, the aim of the people being more honorable than that of the nobles, the latter seeking to oppress, the former not to be oppressed. Add to this, that a Prince can never secure himself against a disaffected people, their number being too great, while he may against a disaffected nobility, since their number is small. The worst that a Prince need fear from a disaffected people is that they may desert him, whereas when the nobles are his enemies he has to fear not only that they may desert him but also that they may turn against him; because, as they have greater craft and foresight, they always choose their time to suit their safety, and seek favor with the side they think will win. Again, a Prince must always live with the same people but need not always live with the same nobles, being able to make and unmake these from day to day, and give and take away their authority at his pleasure.

But to make this part of the matter clearer, I say that as regards the nobles there is this first distinction to be made. They either so govern their conduct as to bind themselves wholly to your fortunes, or they do not. Those who so bind themselves, and who are not grasping, should be loved and honored. As to those who do not so bind themselves, there is this further distinction. For the most part they are held back by pusillanimity and a natural defect of courage, in which case you should make use of them, and of those among them more especially who are prudent, for they will do you honor in prosperity, and in adversity give you no cause for fear. But where they abstain from attaching themselves to you of set purpose and for ambitious ends, it is a sign that they are thinking more of themselves than of you, and against such men a Prince should be on his guard, and treat them as though they were declared enemies, for in his adversity they will always help to ruin him.

He who becomes a Prince through the favor of the people should always keep on good terms with them; which it is easy for him to do, since all they ask is not to be oppressed. But he who against the will of the people is made a Prince by the favor of the nobles, must, above all things, seek to conciliate the people, which he readily may by taking them under his protection. For since men who are well treated by one whom they expected to treat them ill feel the more beholden to their benefactor, the people will at once become better disposed to such a Prince when he protects them than if he owed his Princedom to them.

There are many ways in which a Prince may gain the goodwill of the people, but, because these vary with circumstances, no certain rule can be laid down respecting them, and I shall, therefore, say no more about them. But this is the sum of the matter, that it is essential for a Prince to be on a friendly footing with his people since otherwise he will have no resource in adversity.

And what I affirm let no one controvert by citing the old saw that 'he who builds on the people builds on mire,' for that may be true of a private citizen who presumes on his favor with the people, and counts on being rescued by them when overpowered by his enemies or by the magistrates. In such cases a man may often find himself deceived. But when he who builds on the people is a Prince capable of command, of a spirit not to be cast down by ill-fortune, who, while he animates the whole community by his courage and bearing, neglects no prudent precaution, he will not find himself betrayed by the people, but will be seen to have laid his foundations well.

The most critical juncture for Princedoms of this kind, is at the moment when they are about to pass from the popular to the absolute form of government: and as these Princes exercise their authority either directly or through the agency of the magistrates, in the latter case their position is weaker and more hazardous, since they are wholly in the power of those citizens to whom the magistracies are entrusted, who can, and especially in difficult times with the greatest ease, deprive them of their authority, either by opposing or by not obeying them. And in times of peril it is too late for a Prince to assume to himself an absolute authority, for the citizens and subjects who are accustomed to take their orders from the magistrates will not when dangers threaten take them from the Prince, so that at such seasons there will always be very few in whom he can trust. Such Princes, therefore, must not build on what they see in tranquil times when the citizens feel the need of the State. For then everyone is ready to run, to promise, and, danger of death being remote, even to die for the State. But in troubled times, when the State has need of its citizens, few of them are to be found. And the risk of the experiment is the greater in that it can only be made once. Wherefore, a wise Prince should devise means whereby his subjects may at all times, whether favorable or adverse, feel the need of the State and of him, and then they will always be faithful to him.

Chapter IX

How the Strength of Princedoms Should Be Measured

In examining the character of these Princedoms, another circumstance has to be considered, namely, whether the Prince is strong enough, if occasion demands, to stand alone, or whether he needs continual help from others. To make the matter clearer, I pronounce those to be able to stand alone who, with the men and money at their disposal, can get together an army fit to take the field against any assailant; and, conversely, I judge those to be in constant need of help who cannot take the field against their enemies, but are obliged to retire behind their walls, and to defend themselves there. As to the latter there is nothing to be said, except to exhort such Princes to strengthen and fortify the towns in which they dwell, and take no heed of the country outside. For whoever has thoroughly fortified his town, and put himself on such a footing with his subjects as I have already indicated and shall further speak of, will always be attacked with much caution; for men are always averse to enterprises that are attended with difficulty, and it is impossible not to foresee difficulties in attacking a Prince whose town is strongly fortified and who is not hated by his subjects.

A Prince, therefore, who has a strong city, and who does not make himself hated, cannot be attacked, or should he be so, his assailant will come badly off, since human affairs are so variable that it is almost impossible for anyone to keep an army posted for a whole year without interruption of some sort. Should it be objected that if the citizens have possessions outside the town and see them burned they will lose patience, and that self-interest, together with the hardships of a protracted siege, will cause them to forget their loyalty, I answer that a capable and courageous Prince will always overcome these difficulties by holding out hopes to his subjects that the evil will not be of long continuance; by exciting their fears of the enemy's cruelty; and by dexterously silencing those who seem to him too forward in their complaints. Moreover, it is to be expected that the enemy will burn and lay waste the country immediately on their arrival, at a time when men's minds are still heated and resolute for defense. And for this very reason the Prince has less to fear because after a few days, when the first ardor has abated, the injury is already done and suffered and cannot be undone; and the people will now, all the more readily, make common cause with their Prince from his seeming to be under obligations to them, their houses having been burned and their lands wasted in his defense. For it is the nature of men to incur obligation as much by the benefits they render as by those they receive.

If the whole matter be well considered, it ought not to be difficult for a prudent Prince, both at the outset and afterwards, to maintain the spirits of his subjects during a siege; provided always that provisions and other means of defense do not run short.

CHAPTER X

Of Soldiers and Mercenaries

The arms with which a Prince defends his State are either his own subjects, or they are mercenaries, or they are auxiliaries, or they are partly one and partly another. Mercenaries and auxiliaries are at once useless and dangerous, and he who holds his State by means of mercenary troops can never be solidly or securely seated. For such troops are disunited, ambitious, insubordinate, treacherous, insolent among friends, cowardly before foes, and without fear of God or faith with man. Whenever they are attacked defeat follows; so that in peace you are plundered by them, in war by your enemies. And this is because they have no tie or motive to keep them in the field beyond their paltry pay, in return for which it would be too much to expect them to give their lives. They are ready enough, therefore, to be your soldiers while you are at peace, but when war is declared they make off and disappear. I ought to have little difficulty in getting this believed, for the present ruin of Italy is due to no other cause than her having for many years trusted to mercenaries, who though heretofore they may have helped the fortunes of some one man, and made a show of strength when matched with one another, have always revealed themselves in their true colors so soon as foreign enemies appeared.

The second sort of unprofitable arms are auxiliaries, by whom I mean troops brought to help and protect you by a potentate whom you summon to your aid; as when in recent times, Pope Julius II, observing the pitiful behavior of his mercenaries at the enterprise of Ferrara, betook himself to auxiliaries, and arranged with Ferdinand of Spain to be supplied with horse and foot soldiers.*

Auxiliaries may be excellent and useful soldiers for themselves, but are always hurtful to him who calls them in; for if they are defeated, he is undone; if victorious, he becomes their prisoner. Ancient histories abound with instances of this.

Let him, therefore, who would deprive himself of every chance of success, have recourse to auxiliaries, these being far more dangerous than mercenary arms, bringing ruin with them ready made. For they are united, and wholly under the control of their own officers; whereas, before mercenaries, even after gaining a victory, can do you hurt, longer time and better opportunities are needed; because, as they are made up of separate companies, raised and paid by you, he whom you place in command cannot at once acquire such authority over them as will be injurious to you. In short, with mercenaries your greatest danger is from their inertness and cowardice,

---

* Julius was later forced to make territorial concessions to Ferdinand. —MH

with auxiliaries from their valor. Wise Princes, therefore, have always eschewed these arms, and trusted rather to their own, and have preferred defeat with the latter to victory with the former, counting that as no true victory which is gained by foreign aid.

CHAPTER XI

The Prince and Military Affairs

A Prince, therefore, should have no care or thought other than for war, and for the regulations and training it requires, and should apply himself exclusively to this as his peculiar province; for war is the sole art looked for in one who rules, and is of such efficacy that it not merely maintains those who are born Princes, but often enables men to rise to that eminence from a private station; while, on the other hand, we often see that when Princes devote themselves rather to pleasure than to arms, they lose their dominions. And as neglect of this art is the prime cause of such calamities, to be proficient in it is the surest way to acquire power.

Between an armed and an unarmed man no proportion holds, and it is contrary to reason to expect that the armed man should voluntarily submit to him who is unarmed, or that the unarmed man should stand secure among armed retainers. For with contempt on one side and distrust on the other it is impossible that men should work well together. Wherefore, as has already been said, a Prince who is ignorant of military affairs, besides other disadvantages, can neither be respected by his soldiers, nor can he trust them. A Prince, therefore, ought never to allow his attention to be diverted from warlike pursuits, and should occupy himself with them even more in peace than in war. This he can do in two ways, by practice or by study.

As to the practice, he ought, besides keeping his soldiers well trained and disciplined, to be constantly engaged in the chase, that he may inure his body to hardships and fatigue, and gain at the same time a knowledge of places, by observing how the mountains slope, the valleys open, and the plains spread; acquainting himself with the characters of rivers and marshes, and giving the greatest attention to this subject. Such knowledge is useful to him in two ways; for first, he learns thereby to know his own country, and to understand better how it may be defended; and next, from his familiar acquaintance with its localities, he readily comprehends the character of other districts when obliged to observe them for the first time. For the hills, valleys, plains, rivers, and marshes of Tuscany, for example, have a certain resemblance to those elsewhere; so that from a knowledge of the natural features of that province, similar knowledge in respect of other provinces may readily be gained. The Prince who is wanting in this kind of knowledge, is wanting in the first qualification of a good captain for by it he is taught how to surprise an enemy, how to choose an encampment, how to lead his army on a march, how to array it for battle, and how to post it to the best advantage for a siege.

Among the commendations that Philopoemen, Prince of the Achaeans, has received from historians is this: that in times of peace he was always thinking of methods of warfare, so that when walking in the country with his friends he would often stop and talk with them on the subject. "If the enemy," he would say, "were posted on that hill, and we found ourselves here with our army, which of us would have the better position? How could we most safely and in the best order advance to meet them? If we had to retreat, what direction should we take? If they retired, how should we pursue?" In this way he put to his friends, as he went along, all the contingencies that can befall an army. He listened to their opinions, stated his own, and supported them with reasons; and from his being constantly occupied with such meditations, it resulted, that when in actual command no complication could ever present itself with which he was not prepared to deal.

As to the mental training of which we have spoken, a Prince should read histories, and in these should note the actions of great men, observe how they conducted themselves in their wars, and examine the causes of their victories and defeats. And above all, he should, as many great men of past ages have done, assume for his models those persons who before his time have been renowned and celebrated, whose deeds and achievements he should constantly keep in mind.

A wise Prince, therefore, should pursue such methods as these, never resting idle in times of peace but strenuously seeking to turn them to account, so that he may derive strength from them in the hour of danger, and find himself ready should Fortune turn against him.

CHAPTER XII

Better to Be Loved or Feared?

I say that every Prince should desire to be accounted merciful and not cruel. Nevertheless, he should be on his guard against the abuse of this quality of mercy.

A Prince should disregard the reproach of being thought cruel where it enables him to keep his subjects united and obedient. For he who quells disorder by a very few signal examples will in the end be more merciful than he who from too great leniency permits things to take their course and so to result in pillage and bloodshed; for these hurt the whole State, whereas the severities of the Prince injure individuals only. And for a new Prince, of all others, it is impossible to escape a name for cruelty, since new States are full of dangers.

Nevertheless, the new Prince should not be too ready of belief, nor too easily set in motion; nor should he himself be the first to raise alarms; but should so temper prudence with kindliness that too great confidence in others shall not throw him off his guard nor groundless distrust render him insupportable.

And here comes in the question whether it is better to be loved rather than feared, or feared rather than loved. It might perhaps be answered that we should wish to be

both; but since love and fear can hardly exist together, if
we must choose between them, it is far safer to be feared
than loved. For of men it may generally be affirmed that
they are thankless, fickle, false, studious to avoid danger,
greedy of gain, devoted to you while you are able to confer
benefits upon them, and ready, as I said before, while danger is distant, to shed their blood, and sacrifice their property, their lives, and their children for you; but in the hour
of need they turn against you. The Prince, therefore, who
without otherwise securing himself builds wholly on their
professions is undone. For the friendships which we buy
with a price, and do not gain by greatness and nobility of
character, though they be fairly earned are not made good,
but fail us when we have occasion to use them.

Moreover, men are less careful how they offend him
who makes himself loved than him who makes himself
feared. For love is held by the tie of obligation, which,
because men are a sorry breed, is broken on every whisper
of private interest; but fear is bound by the apprehension of
punishment which never relaxes its grasp.

Nevertheless a Prince should inspire fear in such a fash-
ion that if he do not win love he may escape hate. For a man
may very well be feared and yet not hated, and this will
be the case so long as he does not meddle with the property or with the women of his citizens and subjects. And
if constrained to put any to death, he should do so only
when there is manifest cause or reasonable justification.
But, above all, he must abstain from seizing the property of

others. For men will sooner forget the death of their father than the loss of their estate. Moreover, pretexts for confiscation are difficult to find, and he who has once begun to live by pillaging always finds reasons for taking what is not his; whereas reasons for shedding blood are fewer and sooner exhausted.

Among other things remarkable in Hannibal, this has been noted: that having a very great army, made up of men of many different nations and brought to fight in a foreign country, no dissension ever arose among the soldiers themselves, nor any mutiny against their leader, either in his good or in his evil fortunes. This we can only ascribe to the transcendent cruelty, which, joined with numberless great qualities, rendered him at once venerable and terrible in the eyes of his soldiers, for without this reputation for cruelty these other virtues would not have produced the like results.

CHAPTER XIII

Truth and Deception

E veryone understands how praiseworthy it is in a Prince to maintain trust, and to live uprightly and not craftily. Nevertheless, we see from what has taken place in our own days that Princes who have set little store by their word, but have known how to overreach men by their cunning, have accomplished great things, and in the end got the better of those who trusted to honest dealing.

Be it known, then, that there are two ways of contending, one in accordance with the laws, the other by force; the first of which is proper to men, the second to beasts. But since the first method is often ineffectual, it becomes necessary to resort to the second. A Prince should, therefore, understand how to use well both the man and the beast. And this lesson has been covertly taught by the ancient writers who relate how Achilles and many others of these old Princes were given over to be brought up and trained by Chiron the Centaur; the only meaning of their having for an instructor one who was half man and half beast is that it is necessary for a Prince to know how to use both natures, and that the one without the other has no stability.

But since a Prince should know how to use the beast's nature wisely, he ought of beasts to choose both the lion and the fox; for the lion cannot guard himself from the traps nor the fox from wolves. He must therefore be a fox to discern traps and a lion to drive off wolves.

To rely wholly on the lion is unwise; and for this reason a prudent Prince neither can nor ought to keep his word when to keep it is hurtful to him, and the causes which led him to pledge it are removed. If all men were good this would not be good advice, but since they are dishonest and do not keep faith with you, you in return need not keep faith with them; and no prince was ever at a loss for plausible reasons to cloak a breach of faith. Of this numberless recent instances could be given, and it might be shown how many solemn treaties and engagements have been rendered inoperative and idle through want of faith in Princes, and that he who was best known to play the fox has had the best success.

It is necessary, indeed, to put a good color on this nature, and to be skillful in simulating and dissembling. But men are so simple, and governed so absolutely by their present needs, that he who wishes to deceive will never fail in finding willing dupes.

And you are to understand that a Prince, and most of all a new Prince, cannot observe all those rules of conduct in respect whereof men are accounted good, being often forced, in order to preserve his Princedom, to act in opposition to good faith, charity, humanity, and religion. He must therefore keep his mind ready to shift as the winds and tides of Fortune turn, and, as I have already said, he ought not to quit good courses if he can help it, but should know how to follow evil courses if he must.

A Prince should therefore be very careful that nothing ever escapes his lips that does not make him seem the embodiment of mercy, good faith, integrity, humanity, and religion. And there is no virtue which it is more necessary for him to seem to possess than this last; because men in general judge rather by the eye than by the hand, for everyone can see but few can touch. Everyone sees what you seem, but few know what you are, and these few dare not oppose themselves to the opinion of the many who have the majesty of the State to back them up.

Moreover, in the actions of all men, and most of all of Princes, where there is no tribunal to which we can appeal we look to results. Wherefore if a Prince succeeds in establishing and maintaining his authority the means will always be judged honorable and be approved by everyone. For the vulgar are always taken by appearances and by results, and the world is made up of the vulgar, the few only finding room when the many have no longer ground to stand on.

A certain Prince of our own days, whose name it is as well not to mention, is always preaching peace and good faith, although the mortal enemy of both; and both, had he practiced them as he preaches them, would, oftener than once, have lost him his kingdom and authority.

CHAPTER XIV

How to Avert Conspiracies

A Prince should consider how he may avoid such courses as would make him hated or despised; and that whenever he succeeds in keeping clear of these, he has performed his part, and runs no risk though he incur other infamies.

A Prince, as I have said before, sooner becomes hated by being rapacious and by interfering with the property and with the women of his subjects than in any other way. From these, therefore, he should abstain. For so long as neither their property nor their honor are touched the mass of mankind live contentedly, and the Prince has only to cope with the ambition of a few, which can in many ways and easily be kept within bounds.

A Prince is despised when he is seen to be fickle, frivolous, effeminate, pusillanimous, or irresolute, against which defects he ought therefore most carefully to guard, striving so to bear himself that greatness, courage, wisdom, and strength may appear in all his actions. In his private dealings with his subjects his decisions should be irrevocable, and his reputation such that no one would dream of overreaching or cajoling him.

The Prince who inspires such an opinion of himself is greatly esteemed, and against one who is greatly esteemed conspiracy is difficult; nor, when he is known to be an excellent Prince and held in reverence by his subjects, will it be easy to attack him. For a Prince is exposed to two dangers: from within in respect of his subjects, and from without in respect of foreign powers. Against the latter he will defend himself with good arms and good allies, and if he have good arms he will always have good allies; and when things are settled abroad, they will always be settled at home, unless disturbed by conspiracies; and even should there be hostility from without, if he has taken those measures, and has lived in the way I have recommended, and if he never abandons hope, he will withstand every attack.

As regards his own subjects, when affairs are quiet abroad, he has to fear they may engage in secret plots; against which a Prince best secures himself when he escapes being hated or despised, and keeps on good terms with his people; and this, as I have already shown, is essential. Not to be hated or despised by the body of his subjects is one of the surest safeguards that a Prince can have against conspiracy. For he who conspires always reckons on pleasing the people by putting the Prince to death; but when he sees that instead of pleasing he will offend them, he cannot summon courage to carry out his design. For the difficulties that attend conspirators are infinite, and we know from experience that while there have been many conspiracies, few of them have succeeded.

He who conspires cannot do so alone, nor can he assume as his companions any save those whom he believes to be discontented; but so soon as you impart your design to a discontented man, you supply him with the means of removing his discontent, since by betraying you he can procure for himself every advantage; so that seeing on the one hand certain gain and on the other a doubtful and dangerous risk, he must either be a rare friend to you or the mortal enemy of his Prince, if he keep your secret.

To put the matter shortly, I say that on the side of the conspirator there are distrust, jealousy, and dread of punishment to deter him; while on the side of the Prince there are the laws, the majesty of the throne, the protection of friends and of the government to defend him, to which if the general goodwill of the people be added, it is hardly possible that any should be rash enough to conspire. For while in ordinary cases, the conspirator has ground for fear only before the execution of his villainy, in this case he has also cause to fear after the crime has been perpetrated since he has the people for his enemy and is thus cut off from every hope of shelter.

In brief, a Prince has little to fear from conspiracies when his subjects are well disposed towards him; but when they are hostile and hold him in detestation he has then reason to fear everything and everyone. And well ordered

States and wise Princes have provided with extreme care that the nobility shall not be driven to desperation, and that the commons shall be kept satisfied and contented; for this is one of the most important matters that a Prince must look to.

Chapter XV

How a Prince
Should Defend Himself

To govern more securely some Princes have disarmed their subjects, others have kept the towns
subject to them divided by factions; some have
fostered hostility against themselves, others have sought to
gain over those who at the beginning of their reign were
looked on with suspicion; some have built fortresses, others
have dismantled and destroyed them; and though no definite judgment can be pronounced respecting any of these
methods, without regard to the special circumstances of
the State to which it is proposed to apply them, I shall nevertheless speak of them in as comprehensive a way as the
subject will admit.

It has never chanced that any new Prince has disarmed
his subjects. On the contrary, when he has found them
unarmed he has always armed them. For the arms thus
provided become yours, those whom you suspected grow
faithful, while those who were faithful at the first continue
so, and from your subjects become your partisans. And
though all your subjects cannot be armed yet if those of
them whom you arm be treated with marked favor you can

deal more securely with the rest. For the difference which those whom you supply with arms perceive in their treatment will bind them to you, while the others will excuse you recognizing that those who incur greater risk and responsibility merit greater rewards. But by disarming, you at once give offense, since you show your subjects that you distrust them, either as doubting their courage or as doubting their fidelity, each of which imputations begets hatred against you. Moreover, as you cannot maintain yourself without arms you must have recourse to mercenary troops. What these are I have already shown, but even if they were good, they could never avail to defend you at once against powerful enemies abroad and against subjects whom you distrust. Wherefore, as I have said already, new Princes in new Princedoms have always provided for their being armed; and of instances of this History is full.

But when a Prince acquires a new State, which thus becomes joined on like a limb to his old possessions, he must disarm its inhabitants, except such of them as have taken part with him while he was acquiring it; and even these, as time and occasion serve, he should seek to render soft and effeminate; and he must so manage matters that all the arms of the new State shall be in the hands of his own soldiers who have served under him in his ancient dominions.

I do not believe that divisions purposely caused can ever lead to good; on the contrary, when an enemy approaches, divided cities are lost at once, for the weaker faction will always side with the invader, and the other will not be able to stand alone.

Moreover methods like these argue weakness in a Prince, for under a strong government divisions would never be permitted, since they are profitable only in time of peace as an expedient whereby subjects may be more easily managed; but when war breaks out their insufficiency is demonstrated.

It has been customary for Princes, with a view to hold their dominions more securely, to build fortresses which might serve as a curb and restraint on such as have designs against them, and as a safe refuge against a first onset. I approve this custom, because it has been followed from the earliest times.

Fortresses are useful or not according to circumstances, and if in one way they benefit, in another they injure you. We may state the case thus: the Prince who is more afraid of his subjects than of strangers ought to build fortresses, while he who is more afraid of strangers than of his subjects should leave them alone.

All considerations taken into account, I shall applaud him who builds fortresses and him who does not; but I shall blame him who, trusting in them, reckons it a light thing to be held in hatred by his people.

Chapter XVI

How a Prince Should Preserve His Reputation

Nothing makes a Prince so well thought of as to undertake great enterprises and give striking proofs of his capacity.

It greatly profits a Prince in conducting the internal government of his State to follow striking methods. The remarkable actions of anyone in civil life, whether for good or for evil, afford him notability; and to choose such ways of rewarding and punishing cannot fail to be much spoken of. But above all, he should strive by all his actions to inspire a sense of his greatness and goodness.

A Prince is likewise esteemed who is a stanch friend and a thorough foe, that is to say, who without reserve openly declares for one against another, this being always a more advantageous course than to stand neutral. For supposing two of your powerful neighbors come to blows, it must either be that you have, or have not, reason to fear the one who comes off victorious. In either case it will always be well for you to declare yourself, and join in frankly with one side or other. For should you fail to do so you are certain, in the former of the cases put, to become the prey of the victor to the satisfaction and delight of the vanquished, and no reason or circumstance that you may plead will avail to shield or shelter you; for the victor dislikes doubtful friends, and such as will not help him at a pinch; and the vanquished will have nothing to say to you, since you would not share his fortunes sword in hand.

A Prince should be careful never to join with one stronger than himself in attacking others, unless he is driven to it by necessity. For if he whom you join prevails, you are at his mercy; and Princes, so far as in them lies, should avoid placing themselves at the mercy of others.

A Prince should show himself a patron of merit, and should honor those who excel in every art. He ought accordingly to encourage his subjects by enabling them to pursue their callings, whether mercantile, agricultural, or any other, in security, so that this man shall not be deterred from beautifying his possessions from the apprehension that they may be taken from him, or that other refrain from opening a trade through fear of taxes; and he should provide rewards for those who desire so to employ themselves, and for all who are disposed in any way to add to the greatness of his City or State.

He ought, moreover, at suitable seasons of the year to entertain the people with festivals and shows. And because all cities are divided into guilds and companies, he should show attention to these societies, and sometimes take part in their meetings, offering an example of courtesy and munificence, but always maintaining the dignity of his station, which must under no circumstances be compromised.

CHAPTER XVII

A Prince's Court

The choice of Ministers is a matter of no small moment to a Prince. Whether they shall be good or not depends on his prudence, so that the readiest conjecture we can form of the character and sagacity of a Prince is from seeing what sort of men he has about him. When they are at once capable and faithful, we may always account him wise, since he has known to recognize their merit and to retain their fidelity. But if they be otherwise, we must pronounce unfavorably of him, since he has committed a first fault in making this selection.

There are three scales of intelligence, one which understands by itself, a second which understands what it is shown by others, and a third which understands neither by itself nor by the showing of others, the first of which is most excellent, the second good, but the third worthless.

As to how a Prince is to know his Minister, this unerring rule may be laid down. When you see a Minister thinking more of himself than of you, and in all his actions seeking his own ends, that man can never be a good Minister or one that you can trust. For he who has the charge of the State committed to him, ought not to think of himself, but only of his Prince, and should never bring to the notice of the latter what does not directly concern him. On the other hand, to keep his Minister good, the Prince should be considerate of him, dignifying him, enriching him, binding him to himself by benefits, and sharing with him the honors as well as the burdens of the State, so that the abundant honors and wealth bestowed upon him may divert him from seeking them at other hands; while the great responsibilities wherewith he is charged may lead him to dread change, knowing that he cannot stand alone without his master's support. When Prince and Minister are upon this footing they can mutually trust one another; but when the contrary is the case, it will always fare ill with one or other of them.

Chapter XVIII

Flatterers Should Be Shunned

One error into which Princes, unless very prudent or very fortunate in their choice of friends, are apt to fall, is of so great importance that I must not pass it over. I mean in respect of flatterers. These abound in Courts, because men take such pleasure in their own concerns, and so deceive themselves with regard to them, that they can hardly escape this plague; while even in the effort to escape it there is risk of their incurring contempt.

For there is no way to guard against flattery but by letting it be seen that you take no offense in hearing the truth: but when everyone is free to tell you the truth respect falls short. Wherefore a prudent Prince should follow a middle course, by choosing certain discreet men from among his subjects, and allowing them alone free leave to speak their minds on any matter on which he asks their opinion, and on none other. But he ought to ask their opinion on everything, and after hearing what they have to say, should reflect and judge for himself. And with these counselors collectively, and with each of them separately, his bearing should be such, that each and all of them may know that the more freely they declare their thoughts the better they will be liked. Besides these, the Prince should hearken to no others, but should follow the course determined on, and afterwards adhere firmly to his resolves. Whoever acts otherwise is either undone by flatterers, or from continually vacillating as opinions vary, comes to be held in light esteem.

A Prince ought always to take counsel, but at such times and reasons only as he himself pleases, and not when it pleases others; nay, he should discourage every one from obtruding advice on matters on which it is not sought. But he should be free in asking advice, and afterwards as regards the matters on which he has asked it, a patient hearer of the truth, and even displeased should he perceive that any one, from whatever motive, keeps it back.

But those who think that every Prince who has a name for prudence owes it to the wise counselors he has around him, and not to any merit of his own, are certainly mistaken; since it is an unerring rule and of universal application that a Prince who is not wise himself cannot be well advised by others, unless by chance he surrender himself to be wholly governed by some one adviser who happens to be supremely prudent; in which case he may, indeed, be well advised; but not for long, since such an adviser will soon deprive him of his Government. If he listen to a multitude of advisers, the Prince who is not wise will never have consistent counsels, nor will he know of himself how to reconcile them. Each of his counselors will study his own advantage, and the Prince will be unable to detect or correct them. Nor could it well be otherwise, for men will

always grow rogues on your hands unless they find themselves under a necessity to be honest.

Hence it follows that good counsels, whenever they
come, have their origin in the prudence of the Prince, and
not the prudence of the Prince in wise counsels.

CHAPTER XIX

The Role of Fortune

I am not ignorant that many have been and are of the opinion that human affairs are so governed by Fortune and by God that men cannot alter them by any prudence of theirs, and indeed have no remedy against them, and for this reason have come to think that it is not worthwhile to labour much about anything, but that they must leave everything to be determined by chance.

Often when I turn the matter over, I am in part inclined to agree with this opinion, which has had readier acceptance in our own times from the great changes in things which we have seen and everyday see happen contrary to all human expectation. Nevertheless, that our freewill be not wholly set aside, I think it may be the case that Fortune is the mistress of one half our actions, and yet leaves the control of the other half, or a little less, to ourselves. And I would liken her to one of those wild torrents which, when angry, overflow the plains, sweep away trees and houses, and carry off soil from one bank to throw it down upon the other. Everyone flees before them, and yields to their fury without the least power to resist. And yet, though this be their nature, it does not follow that in seasons of fair weather men cannot, by constructing dams and barriers, take such precautions as will cause them when again in flood to pass off by some artificial channel, or at least prevent their course from being so uncontrolled and destructive. And so it is with Fortune, who displays her might where there is no organized strength to resist her, and directs her onset where she knows that there is neither barrier nor embankment to confine her.

I note that one day we see a Prince prospering and the next day overthrown, without detecting any change in his nature or character. This, I believe, comes chiefly from a cause already dwelt upon, namely, that a Prince who rests wholly on Fortune is ruined when she changes. Moreover, I believe that he will prosper most whose mode of acting best adapts itself to the character of the times; and conversely that he will be unprosperous with whose mode of acting the times do not accord. For we see that men in these matters which lead to the end that each has before him, namely, glory and wealth, proceed by different ways, one with caution, another with impetuosity, one with violence, another with subtlety, one with patience, another with its contrary; and that by one or other of these different courses each may succeed.

Again, of two who act cautiously, you shall find that one attains his end, the other not, and that two of different temperament, the one cautious, the other impetuous, are equally successful. All which happens from no other cause than that the character of the times accords or does not accord with their methods of acting. And hence it comes, as I have already said, that two operating differently arrive at the same result, and two operating similarly, the one succeeds and the other not. On this likewise depend the vicissitudes of Fortune. For if to one who conducts himself with caution and patience, time and circumstances are propitious, so that his method of acting is good, he goes on prospering; but if these change he is ruined, because he does not change his method of acting.

For no man is found so prudent as to know how to adapt himself to these changes, both because he cannot deviate from the course to which nature inclines him, and because, having always prospered while adhering to one path, he cannot be persuaded that it would be well for him to forsake it. And so when occasion requires the cautious man to act impetuously, he cannot do so and is undone: whereas, had he changed his nature with time and circumstances, his fortune would have been unchanged.

To be brief, I say that since Fortune changes and men stand fixed in their old ways, they are prosperous so long as there is congruity between them, and the reverse when there is not. Of this, however, I am well persuaded, that it is better to be impetuous than cautious. For Fortune to be kept under must be beaten and roughly handled; and we see that she suffers herself to be more readily mastered by those who so treat her than by those who are more timid in their approaches. And always she favors the young, because they are less scrupulous and fiercer, and command her with greater audacity.

CHAPTER XX

Aphorisms from *The Prince*

"One change always leaves a dovetail into which another will fit."

"Men are either to be kindly treated or utterly crushed since they can revenge lighter injuries but not graver."

"The wise man should always follow the roads that have been trodden by the great, and imitate those who have most excelled."

"Take aim much above the destined mark."

"He who is less beholden to Fortune has often in the end the better success."

"Those who come to the Princedom by virtuous paths acquire with difficulty but keep with ease."

"It should be borne in mind that the temper of the multitude is fickle, and that while it is easy to persuade them of a thing, it is hard to fix them in that persuasion."

"He who does not lay his foundations at first, may, if he be of great ability, succeed in laying them afterwards, though with inconvenience to the builder and risk to the building."

"A Prince can never secure himself against a disaffected people, their number being too great, while he may against a disaffected nobility, since their number is small."

"Men are always averse to enterprises that are attended with difficulty."

"Mercenaries and auxiliaries are at once useless and dangerous, and he who holds his State by means of mercenary troops can never be solidly or securely seated."

"A Prince ought never to allow his attention to be diverted from warlike pursuits, and should occupy himself with them even more in peace than in war."

"Many Republics and Princedoms have been imagined that were never seen or known to exist in reality."

"If we must choose between them, it is far safer to be feared than loved."

"If a man have good arms he will always have good allies."

"I do not believe that divisions purposely caused can ever lead to good."

"A Prince should show himself a patron of merit."

"The readiest conjecture we can form of the character and sagacity of a Prince is from seeing what sort of men he has about him."

"A Prince who is not wise himself cannot be well advised by others."

"A Prince who rests wholly on Fortune is ruined when she changes."

"It is better to be impetuous than cautious. Fortune suffers herself to be more readily mastered by those who so treat her than by those who are timid in their approaches."

About the Author

Born in Florence in 1469, NICCOLÒ MACHIAVELLI was a widely travelled and deeply read diplomatic envoy for Italy's royal court. Also a politician, historian, philosopher, humanist, writer, playwright, and poet, he has been called the founder of modern political science for his efforts to arrive at a cause-and-effect formula for how to attain and hold power and conduct statecraft. Machiavelli's classic *The Prince* was posthumously published in 1532. It was made up of earlier papers and letters that he had prepared for his royal patrons. A short work of considerable innovation, *The Prince* is one of the most enduring and widely read pieces of Renaissance literature. Although the term "Machiavellian" came to refer to actions or people characterized by cunning ruthlessness, contemporary critics and scholars are taking fuller note of Machiavelli's ethics and reformist sympathies. The writer died in Florence at age 58 in 1527.

THE ART
OF WAR

THE ART
OF WAR

by Sun Tzu

History's Greatest Work on Strategy—
Now in a Special Condensation

Abridged and Introduced
by Mitch Horowitz

THE CONDENSED CLASSICS LIBRARY™

Contents

Introduction

———⋅—⋅———

The Unlikeliest Classic

by Mitch Horowitz

Since its first creditable English translation in 1910, the ancient Chinese martial text *The Art of War* has enthralled Western readers. First gaining the attention of military officers, sinologists, martial artists, and strategy aficionados, *The Art of War* is today read by business executives, athletes, artists, and seekers from across the self-help spectrum. This is a surprising destiny for a work on ancient warfare estimated to be written around 500 BC by Zhou dynasty general Sun Tzu, an honorific title meaning "Master Sun." Very little is known about the author other than a historical consensus that such a figure actually existed as a commander in the dynastic emperor's army.

What, then, accounts for the enduring popularity of a text that might have been conscripted to obscurity in the West?

Like the best writing from the Taoist tradition, *The Art of War* is exquisitely simple, practical, and clear. Its insights into life and its inevitable conflicts are so organic and sound—Taoism is based on aligning with the natural order of things—that many people who have never been on a battlefield are immediately drawn into wanting to apply Sun Tzu's maxims to daily life.

Indeed, this gentle condensation is intended to highlight those aphorisms and lessons that have the broadest general applicability. I have no doubt that as you experience this volume you will immediately discover ideas that you want to note and use. This is because Sun Tzu's genius as a writer is to return us to natural principles—things that we may have once understood intuitively but lost in superfluous and speculative analysis, another of life's inevitabilities.

I have based this abridgment on the aforementioned and invaluable 1910 English translation by British sinologist Lionel Giles. Giles' translation has stood up with remarkable relevance over the past century. Rather than laden his words with the flourish of late-Victorian prose, Giles honored the starkness and sparseness of the original work. I have occasionally altered an obscure or antiquated term, but, overall, the economy and elegance of Giles' translation is an art form in itself, and deserves to be honored as such.

Why then a condensation at all? In some instances, Sun Tzu, a working military commander, necessarily touched upon battlefield intricacies—such as the fine points of terrain or attacking the enemy with fire—that prove less immediately applicable to modern life than his observations on the movements and motives of men. In a few spots I also add a clarifying note to bring out Sun Tzu's broader points.

I ask the reader to take special note of Sun Tzu's frequent references to adhering to the natural landscape. It is a classically Taoist approach to blend with the curvature and qualities of one's surroundings—to find your place in the organic order of things. Within the Vedic tradition this is sometimes called dharma. Transcendentalist philosopher Ralph Waldo Emerson also notes the need to cycle yourself with the patterns of nature. As the great Hermetic dictum put it: "As above, so below."

Another key to Sun Tzu's popularity is the manner in which he unlocks the universality of true principles. What applies in warfare, if authentic, must apply to other areas of life. Human nature is consistent. So are the ebb and flow of events, on both macro and intimate levels. Be on the watch for this principle throughout the text.

Another central aspect of Sun Tzu's thought—again in harmony with Taoism—is that the greatest warrior prevails without ever fighting. If a fighter has observed conditions, deciphered the enemy, and diligently prepared and marshaled his forces, the ideal is to overwhelm his foe without shooting a single arrow. "Supreme excellence," Sun Tzu writes, "consists in breaking the enemy's resistance without fighting."

If an attack does prove necessary, it should be launched with irresistible force, like a seismic shifting of the earth. After your enemy's defeat, quickly return to normalcy. "In war then," the master writes, "let your object be victory, not lengthy campaigns." Sun Tzu warns against protracted operations. "There is no instance of a country having benefited from prolonged warfare," he writes.

Rather than seek glory, Sun Tzu counsels that the excellent commander practices subtlety, inscrutability, watchfulness, and flexibility. The good fighter, he writes, should be like water: dwelling unnoticed at his enemy's lowest depths and then striking with overwhelming power at his weakest points, the way a torrent of water rushes downhill. This constitutes ideal preparation and formation for attack: practice patience, carefully study the enemy, know his limits and strengths and your own, never be lured or tricked into battle—and then strike with ferocity. And never fight unless victory is assured.

If I had to put *The Art of War* into a nutshell, I would use this one of the master's maxims: "Let your plans be dark and impenetrable as night, and when you move, fall like a thunderbolt."

In a sense, *The Art of War* is about unlearning the complexities of life and returning to the simple and true. This voice from millennia ago can teach us how to strip away obfuscation. May its wisdom bring you your highest effectiveness.

Chapter I

Laying Plans

S un Tzu said: The art of war is of vital importance to the State.

It is a matter of life and death, a road either to safety or to ruin. Hence, it is a subject of inquiry that can on no account be neglected.

The art of war, then, is governed by five constant factors, to be taken into account in one's deliberations when seeking to determine the conditions obtaining in the field.

These are:

(1) The Moral Law;

(2) Heaven;

(3) Earth;

(4) The Commander;

(5) Method and Discipline.

The Moral Law causes the people to be in complete accord with their ruler, so that they will follow him regardless of their lives, undismayed by any danger.

Heaven signifies night and day, cold and heat, times and seasons.

Earth comprises distances, great and small; danger and security; open ground and narrow passes; the chances of life and death.

The Commander stands for the virtues of wisdom, sincerity, benevolence, courage, and strictness.

By method and discipline are to be understood the marshaling of the army in its proper subdivisions, the graduations of rank among the officers, the maintenance of roads by which supplies may reach the army, and the control of military expenditure.

These five heads should be familiar to every general: he who knows them will be victorious; he who knows them not will fail.

Therefore, in your deliberations, when seeking to determine the military conditions, let them be made the basis of a comparison, in this way:

(1) Which of the two sovereigns is imbued with the Moral Law?

(2) Which of the two generals has most ability?

(3) With whom lie the advantages derived from Heaven and Earth?

(4) On which side is discipline most rigorously enforced?

(5) Which army is stronger?

(6) On which side are officers and men more highly trained?

(7) In which army is there the greater constancy both in reward and punishment?

By means of these seven considerations I can forecast victory or defeat.

The general that hearkens to my counsel and acts upon it, will conquer: let such a one be retained in command! The general that hearkens not to my counsel nor acts upon it, will suffer defeat—let such a one be dismissed!

While heeding the profit of my counsel, avail yourself also of any helpful circumstances over and beyond the ordinary rules.

According as circumstances are favorable, one should modify one's plans.

All warfare is based on deception.

Hence, when able to attack, we must seem unable; when using our forces, we must seem inactive; when we are near, we must make the enemy believe we are far away; when far away, we must make him believe we are near.

Hold out baits to entice the enemy. Feign disorder, and crush him.

If he is secure at all points, be prepared for him. If he is in superior strength, evade him.

If your opponent is bad-tempered, seek to irritate him. Pretend to be weak, that he may grow arrogant.

If he is at ease, give him no rest. If his forces are united, separate them.

Attack him where he is unprepared, appear where you are not expected.

These military devices, leading to victory, must not be divulged beforehand.

Now the general who wins a battle makes many calculations in his temple ere the battle is fought. The general who loses a battle makes but few calculations beforehand. Thus do many calculations lead to victory, and few calculations to defeat: how much more no calculation at all! It is by attention to this point that I can foresee who is likely to win or lose.

Chapter II

Waging War

When you engage in actual fighting, if victory is long in coming, then men's weapons will grow dull and their ardor will be dampened. If you lay siege to a town, you will exhaust your strength.

Again, if the campaign is protracted, the resources of the State will not be equal to the strain.

Now, when your weapons are dulled, your ardor dampened, your strength exhausted and your treasure spent, other chieftains will spring up to take advantage of your extremity. Then no man, however wise, will be able to avert the consequences that must ensue.

Thus, though we have heard of stupid haste in war, cleverness has never been seen associated with long delays.

There is no instance of a country having benefited from prolonged warfare.

It is only one who is thoroughly acquainted with the evils of war that can thoroughly understand the profitable way of carrying it on.

The skillful soldier does not levy a second tax, neither are his supply-wagons loaded more than twice.

Bring war material with you from home, but forage on the enemy. Thus the army will have food enough for its needs.

Poverty of the State treasury causes an army to be maintained by contributions from a distance. Contributing to maintain an army at a distance causes the people to be impoverished.

On the other hand, the proximity of an army causes prices to go up; and high prices cause the people's substance to be drained away.

When their substance is drained away, the peasantry will be afflicted by heavy exactions.

With this loss of substance and exhaustion of strength, the homes of the people will be stripped bare, and three-tenths of their income will be dissipated; while government expenses for broken chariots, worn-out horses, breast-plates and helmets, bows and arrows, spears and shields, protective mantles, draught-oxen and heavy wagons, will amount to four-tenths of its total revenue.

Hence a wise general makes a point of foraging on the enemy. One cartload of the enemy's provisions is equivalent to twenty of one's own, and likewise a single parcel from his stores is equivalent to twenty from one's own stores.

Now in order to kill the enemy, our men must be roused to anger; that there may be advantage from defeating the enemy, they must have their rewards.

Therefore in chariot fighting, when ten or more chariots have been taken, those should be rewarded who took the first. Our own flags should be substituted for those of the enemy, and the chariots mingled and used in conjunction with ours. The captured soldiers should be kindly treated and kept.

This is called, using the conquered foe to augment one's own strength.

In war, then, let your great object be victory, not lengthy campaigns.

Thus it may be known that the leader of armies is the arbiter of the people's fate, the man on whom it depends whether the nation shall be in peace or in peril.

CHAPTER III

Attack by Stratagem

S un Tzu said: In the practical art of war, the best thing of all is to take the enemy's country whole and intact; to shatter and destroy it is not so good. So, too, it is better to recapture an army entire than to destroy it, to capture a regiment, a detachment or a company entire than to destroy them.

Hence to fight and conquer in all your battles is not supreme excellence; supreme excellence consists in breaking the enemy's resistance without fighting.

Thus the highest form of generalship is to block the enemy's plans; the next best is to prevent the junction of the enemy's forces; the next in order is to attack the enemy's army in the field; and the worst policy of all is to besiege walled cities.

The rule is, not to besiege walled cities if it can possibly be avoided. The preparation of mantlets, movable shelters, and various implements of war, will take up three whole months; and the piling up of mounds over against the walls will take three months more.

The general, unable to control his irritation, will launch his men to the assault like swarming ants, with the result that one-third of his men are slain, while the town still remains untaken. Such are the disastrous effects of a siege.

Therefore the skillful leader subdues the enemy's troops without any fighting; he captures their cities without laying siege to them; he overthrows their kingdom without lengthy operations in the field.

With his forces intact he will dispute the mastery of the Empire, and thus, without losing a man, his triumph will be complete. This is the method of attacking by stratagem.

It is the rule in war, if our forces are ten to the enemy's one, to surround him; if five to one, to attack him; if twice as numerous, to divide our army into two.

If equally matched, we can offer battle; if slightly inferior in numbers, we can avoid the enemy; if quite unequal in every way, we can flee from him.

Hence, though an obstinate fight may be made by a small force, in the end it must be captured by the larger force.

Now the general is the bulwark of the State; if the bulwark is complete at all points, the State will be strong; if the bulwark is defective, the State will be weak.

There are three ways in which a ruler can bring misfortune upon his army:

(1) By commanding the army to advance or to retreat, being ignorant of the fact that it cannot obey. This is called hobbling the army.

(2) By attempting to govern an army in the same way as he administers a kingdom, being ignorant of the condi-

tions which obtain in an army. This causes restlessness in the soldiers' minds.

(3) By employing the officers of his army without discrimination, through ignorance of the military principle of adaptation to circumstances. This shakes the confidence of the soldiers.

But when the army is restless and distrustful, trouble is sure to come from the other feudal princes. This is simply bringing anarchy into the army, and flinging victory away.

Thus we may know that there are five essentials for victory:

(1) He will win who knows when to fight and when not to fight.

(2) He will win who knows how to handle both superior and inferior forces.

(3) He will win whose army is animated by the same spirit throughout all its ranks.

(4) He will win who, prepared himself, waits to take the enemy unprepared.

(5) He will win who has military capacity and is not interfered with by the sovereign.

Hence the saying: If you know the enemy and know yourself, you need not fear the result of a hundred battles. If you know yourself but not the enemy, for every victory gained you will also suffer a defeat. If you know neither the enemy nor yourself, you will succumb in every battle.

Chapter IV

Tactical Dispositions

Sun Tzu said: The good fighters of old first put themselves beyond the possibility of defeat, and then waited for an opportunity of defeating the enemy.

To secure ourselves against defeat lies in our own hands, but the opportunity of defeating the enemy is provided by the enemy himself.

Thus the good fighter is able to secure himself against defeat, but cannot make certain of defeating the enemy.

Hence the saying: One may know how to conquer without being able to do it.*

Security against defeat implies defensive tactics; ability to defeat the enemy means taking the offensive.

Standing on the defensive indicates insufficient strength; attacking, a superabundance of strength.

The general who is skilled in defense hides in the most secret recesses of the earth; he who is skilled in attack flashes forth from the topmost heights of heaven. Thus on the one hand we have ability to protect ourselves; on the other, a victory that is complete.

---

* This is natural law: where two parties are involved the outcome depends on both. —MH

To see victory only when it is within the ken of the common herd is not the acme of excellence.

Neither is it the acme of excellence if you fight and conquer and the whole Empire says, "Well done!"

To lift an autumn hair is no sign of great strength; to see the sun and moon is no sign of sharp sight; to hear the noise of thunder is no sign of a quick ear.

What the ancients called a clever fighter is one who not only wins, but excels in winning with ease.

Hence his victories bring him neither reputation for wisdom nor credit for courage.

He wins his battles by making no mistakes. Making no mistakes is what establishes the certainty of victory, for it means conquering an enemy that is already defeated.

Hence the skillful fighter puts himself into a position which makes defeat impossible, and does not miss the moment for defeating the enemy.

Thus it is that in war the victorious strategist only seeks battle after the victory has been won, whereas he who is destined to defeat first fights and afterwards looks for victory.

The consummate leader cultivates the moral law, and strictly adheres to method and discipline; thus it is in his power to control success.*

---

* It is useful here to note that Sun Tzu adheres not to inspiration, which can come and go, but to "method and discipline," where are permanent.—MH

In respect of military method, we have, firstly, Measurement; secondly, Estimation of quantity; thirdly, Calculation; fourthly, Balancing of chances; fifthly, Victory.

Measurement owes its existence to Earth; Estimation of quantity to Measurement; Calculation to Estimation of quantity; Balancing of chances to Calculation; and Victory to Balancing of chances.

A victorious army opposed to a routed one, is as a pound's weight placed in the scale against a single grain.

The onrush of a conquering force is like the bursting of pent-up waters into a chasm a thousand fathoms deep.

Chapter V

Energy

S un Tzu said: The control of a large force is the same principle as the control of a few men: it is merely a question of dividing up their numbers.

Fighting with a large army under your command is in no way different from fighting with a small one: it is merely a question of instituting signs and signals.

To ensure that your whole army may withstand the brunt of the enemy's attack and remain unshaken—this is effected by maneuvers direct and indirect.

That the impact of your army may be like a grindstone dashed against an egg—this is effected by the science of weak points and strong.

In all fighting, the direct method may be used for joining battle, but indirect methods will be needed in order to secure victory.

Indirect tactics, efficiently applied, are inexhaustible as Heaven and Earth, unending as the flow of rivers and streams; like the sun and moon, they end but to begin anew; like the four seasons, they pass away to return once more.*

---

* This precept should be read and contemplated carefully with the one immediately preceding it.—MH

There are not more than five musical notes, yet the combinations of these five give rise to more melodies than can ever be heard.

There are not more than five primary colors (blue, yellow, red, white, and black), yet in combination they produce more hues than can ever been seen.

There are not more than five cardinal tastes (sour, acrid, salt, sweet, bitter), yet combinations of them yield more flavors than can ever be tasted.

In battle, there are not more than two methods of attack—the direct and the indirect; yet these two in combination give rise to an endless series of maneuvers.

The direct and the indirect lead on to each other in turn. It is like moving in a circle—you never come to an end. Who can exhaust the possibilities of their combination?

The onset of troops is like the rush of a torrent, which will even roll stones along in its course.

The quality of decision is like the well-timed swoop of a falcon, which enables it to strike and destroy its victim.

Therefore the good fighter will be terrible in his onset, and prompt in his decision.

Energy may be likened to the bending of a crossbow; decision, to the releasing of a trigger.

Amid the turmoil and tumult of battle, there may be seeming disorder and yet no real disorder at all; amid confusion and chaos, your array may be without head or tail, yet it will be proof against defeat.

Simulated disorder postulates perfect discipline, simulated fear postulates courage; simulated weakness postulates strength.

Hiding order beneath the cloak of disorder is simply a question of subdivision; concealing courage under a show of timidity presupposes a fund of latent energy; masking strength with weakness is to be effected by tactical dispositions.

Thus one who is skillful at keeping the enemy on the move maintains deceitful appearances, according to which the enemy will act. He sacrifices something, that the enemy may snatch at it.

By holding out baits, he keeps him on the march; then with a body of picked men he lies in wait for him.

The clever combatant looks to the effect of combined energy, and does not require too much from individuals. Hence his ability to pick out the right men and utilize combined energy.*

When he utilizes combined energy, his fighting men become as it were like unto rolling logs or stones. For it is the nature of a log or stone to remain motionless on level ground, and to move when on a slope; if four-cornered, to come to a standstill, but if round-shaped, to go rolling down.

Thus the energy developed by good fighting men is as the momentum of a round stone rolled down a mountain thousands of feet in height.

---

* Sun Tzu is saying that you must not over-rely on any one person or factor.—MH

CHAPTER VI

Weak Points and Strong

un Tzu said: Whoever is first in the field and awaits the coming of the enemy, will be fresh for the fight; whoever is second in the field and has to hasten to battle will arrive exhausted.*

Therefore the clever combatant imposes his will on the enemy, but does not allow the enemy's will to be imposed on him.

By holding out advantages to him, he can cause the enemy to approach of his own accord; or, by inflicting damage, he can make it impossible for the enemy to draw near.

If the enemy is taking his ease, he can harass him; if well supplied with food, he can starve him out; if quietly encamped, he can force him to move.

Appear at points that the enemy must hasten to defend; march swiftly to places where you are not expected.

An army may march great distances without distress, if it marches through country where the enemy is not.

You can be sure of succeeding in your attacks if you only attack places that are undefended. You can ensure the

---

* This is one of Sun Tzu's most practical lessons: always arrive first.—MH

safety of your defense if you only hold positions that cannot be attacked.

Hence that general is skillful in attack whose opponent does not know what to defend; and he is skillful in defense whose opponent does not know what to attack.

O divine art of subtlety and secrecy! Through you we learn to be invisible, through you inaudible; and hence we can hold the enemy's fate in our hands.

You may advance and be absolutely irresistible, if you make for the enemy's weak points; you may retire and be safe from pursuit if your movements are more rapid than those of the enemy.

If we wish to fight, the enemy can be forced to an engagement even though he be sheltered behind a high rampart and a deep ditch. All we need do is attack some other place that he will be obliged to relieve.

If we do not wish to fight, we can prevent the enemy from engaging us even though the lines of our encampment be merely traced out on the ground. All we need do is to throw something odd and unaccountable in his way.

By discovering the enemy's dispositions and remaining invisible ourselves, we can keep our forces concentrated, while the enemy's must be divided.

We can form a single united body, while the enemy must split up into fractions. Hence there will be a whole pitted against separate parts of a whole, which means that we shall be many to the enemy's few.

And if we are able thus to attack an inferior force with a superior one, our opponents will be in dire straits.

The spot where we intend to fight must not be made known; for then the enemy will have to prepare against a possible attack at several different points; and his forces being thus distributed in many directions, the numbers we shall have to face at any given point will be proportionately few.

For should the enemy strengthen his approach, he will weaken his rear; should he strengthen his rear, he will weaken his approach; should he strengthen his left, he will weaken his right; should he strengthen his right, he will weaken his left. If he sends reinforcements everywhere, he will everywhere be weak.

Numerical weakness comes from having to prepare against possible attacks; numerical strength, from compelling our adversary to make these preparations against us.

Knowing the place and the time of the coming battle, we may concentrate from the greatest distances in order to fight.

Though the enemy be stronger in numbers, we may prevent him from fighting. Scheme so as to discover his plans and the likelihood of their success.

Rouse him, and learn the principle of his activity or inactivity. Force him to reveal himself, so as to find out his vulnerable spots.

Carefully compare the opposing army with your own, so that you may know where strength is superabundant and where it is deficient.

In making tactical dispositions, the highest pitch you can attain is to conceal them; conceal your dispositions, and you will be safe from the prying of the subtlest spies, from the machinations of the wisest brains.

How victory may be produced for them out of the enemy's own tactics—that is what the multitude cannot comprehend.

All men can see the tactics whereby I conquer, but what none can see is the strategy out of which victory is evolved.

Do not repeat the tactics that have gained you one victory, but let your methods be regulated by the infinite variety of circumstances.

Military tactics are like unto water; for water in its natural course runs away from high places and hastens downwards.

So in war, the way is to avoid what is strong and to strike at what is weak.

Water shapes its course according to the nature of the ground over which it flows; the soldier works out his victory in relation to the foe that he is facing.*

Therefore, just as water retains no constant shape, so in warfare there are no constant conditions.

He who can modify his tactics in relation to his opponent and thereby succeed in winning, may be called a heaven-born captain.

---

* Sun Tzu is counseling flexibility, morphing, and response to changed circumstances. Do not be rigid.—MH

The five elements (water, fire, wood, metal, earth) are not always equally predominant; the four seasons make way for each other in turn. There are short days and long; the moon has its periods of waning and waxing.

Chapter VII

Maneuvering

S un Tzu said: In war, the general receives his commands from the sovereign.

Having collected an army and concentrated his forces, he must blend and harmonize the different elements thereof before pitching his camp.

After that, comes tactical maneuvering, than which there is nothing more difficult. The difficulty of tactical maneuvering consists in turning the devious into the direct, and misfortune into gain.

Thus, to take a long and circuitous route, after enticing the enemy out of the way, and though starting after him, to contrive to reach the goal before him, shows knowledge of the artifice of DEVIATION.

Maneuvering with an army is advantageous; with an undisciplined multitude, most dangerous.

If you set a fully equipped army to march in order to snatch an advantage, the chances are that you will be too late. On the other hand, to detach a flying column for the purpose involves the sacrifice of its baggage and stores.

Thus, if you order your men to roll up their buff-coats, and make forced marches without halting day or night, covering double the usual distance at a stretch in order to wrest an advantage, the leaders of all your three divisions will fall into the hands of the enemy.

The stronger men will be in front, the jaded ones will fall behind, and on this plan only one-tenth of your army will reach its destination.

If you march long distances to outmaneuver the enemy, you will lose the leader of your first division, and only half your force will reach the goal. Even you modify the long distance, two-thirds of your army will arrive.

Hence it follows that an army without its baggage-train is lost; without provisions it is lost; without bases of supply it is lost.

We cannot enter into alliances until we are acquainted with the designs of our neighbors.

We are not fit to lead an army on the march unless we are familiar with the face of the country—its mountains and forests, its pitfalls and precipices, its marshes and swamps.

We shall be unable to turn natural advantage to account unless we make use of local guides.

In war, practice concealment, and you will succeed.

Whether to concentrate or to divide your troops, must be decided by circumstances.

Let your rapidity be that of the wind, your compactness that of the forest.

In raiding and plundering be like fire, as immovability is like a mountain.

Let your plans be dark and impenetrable as night, and when you move, fall like a thunderbolt.

When you plunder a countryside, let the spoils be divided amongst your men; when you capture new territory, cut it up into allotments for the benefit of the soldiery.

Ponder and deliberate before you make a move.

He will conquer who has learnt the artifice of deviation. Such is the art of maneuvering.

The Book of Army Management says: On the field of battle, the spoken word does not carry far enough: hence the institution of gongs and drums. Nor can ordinary objects be seen clearly enough: hence the institution of banners and flags.

Gongs and drums, banners and flags, are means whereby the ears and eyes of the army may be focused on one particular point.

The army thus forming a single united body, it is impossible either for the brave to advance alone, or for the cowardly to retreat alone. This is the art of handling large masses of men.

In night-fighting, then, make much use of signal-fires and drums, and in fighting by day, of flags and banners, as a means of influencing the ears and eyes of your army.

A whole army may be robbed of its spirit; a commander-in-chief may be robbed of his presence of mind.

Now a soldier's spirit is keenest in the morning; by noonday it has begun to flag; and in the evening, his mind is bent only on returning to camp.

A clever general, therefore, avoids an army when its spirit is keen, but attacks it when it is sluggish and inclined to return. This is the art of studying moods.

Disciplined and calm, to await the appearance of disorder and hubbub amongst the enemy—this is the art of retaining self-possession.

To be near the goal while the enemy is still far from it, to wait at ease while the enemy is toiling and struggling, to be well-fed while the enemy is famished—this is the art of husbanding one's strength.

To refrain from intercepting an enemy whose banners are in perfect order, to refrain from attacking an army drawn up in calm and confident array—this is the art of studying circumstances.

It is a military axiom not to advance uphill against the enemy, nor to oppose him when he comes downhill.

Do not pursue an enemy who simulates flight; do not attack soldiers whose temper is keen.

Do not swallow bait offered by the enemy. Do not interfere with an army that is returning home.

When you surround an army, leave an outlet free. Do not press a desperate foe too hard.*

Such is the art of warfare.

---

* By pressing a desperate foe, and leaving him no way out, you ensure he will fight to the death.—MH

CHAPTER VIII

Variation in Tactics

Sun Tzu said: In war, the general receives his commands from the sovereign, collects his army, and concentrates his forces

When in difficult country, do not encamp. In country where high roads intersect, join hands with your allies. Do not linger in dangerously isolated positions. In hemmed-in situations, you must resort to stratagem. In desperate position, you must fight.

There are roads that must not be followed, armies that must be not attacked, towns that must be besieged, positions that must not be contested, commands of the sovereign that must not be obeyed.

The general who thoroughly understands the advantages that accompany variation of tactics knows how to handle his troops.

The general who does not understand these may be well acquainted with the configuration of the country, yet he will not be able to turn his knowledge to practical account.

So, the student of war who is unversed in the art of war of varying his plans, even though he is acquainted with the Five Advantages, will fail to make the best use of his men.*

Hence in the wise leader's plans, considerations of advantage and of disadvantage will be blended together.

If our expectation of advantage is tempered in this way, we may succeed in accomplishing the essential part of our schemes.

If, on the other hand, in the midst of difficulties we are always ready to seize an advantage, we may extricate ourselves from misfortune.

Reduce the hostile chiefs by inflicting damage on them; and make trouble for them, and keep them constantly engaged; hold out specious allurements, and make them rush to any given point.

The art of war teaches us to rely not on the likelihood of the enemy's not coming, but on our own readiness to receive him; not on the chance of his not attacking, but rather on the fact that we have made our position unassailable. There are five dangerous faults which may affect a general:

(1) Recklessness, which leads to destruction;

(2) cowardice, which leads to capture;

(3) a hasty temper, which can be provoked by insults;

(4) a delicacy of honor which is sensitive to shame;

(5) over-solicitude for his men, which exposes him to worry and trouble.

---

* For the "Five Advantages," see Sun Tzu's note on the "five essentials for victory" in chapter III.—MH

These are the five besetting sins of a general, ruinous to the conduct of war.

When an army is overthrown and its leader slain, the cause will surely be found among these five dangerous faults. Let them be a subject of meditation.

Chapter IX

The Army on the March

Sun Tzu said: We come now to the question of encamping the army, and observing signs of the enemy. Pass quickly over mountains, and keep in the neighborhood of valleys.

Camp in high places, facing the sun. Do not climb heights in order to fight.

After crossing a river, you should get far away from it.

When an invading force crosses a river in its onward march, do not advance to meet it in midstream. It will be best to let half the army get across, and then deliver your attack.

If you are anxious to fight, you should not go to meet the invader near a river that he has to cross.*

Moor your craft higher up than the enemy, and facing the sun. Do not move upstream to meet the enemy.

In crossing saltmarshes, your sole concern should be to get over them quickly, without any delay.

If forced to fight in a saltmarsh, you should have water and grass near you, and get your back to a clump of trees.

---

* In these passages, Sun Tzu is staying that you must exhaust your enemy by enticing him to cross a river.—MH

In dry, level country, take up an easily accessible position with rising ground to your right and on your rear, so that the danger may be in front, and safety lie behind.

All armies prefer high ground to low and sunny places to dark.

If you are careful of your men, and camp on hard ground, the army will be free from disease of every kind, and this will spell victory.

When you come to a hill or a bank, occupy the sunny side, with the slope on your right rear. Thus you will at once act for the benefit of your soldiers and utilize the natural advantages of the ground.

When, in consequence of heavy rains up-country, a river you wish to ford is swollen and flecked with foam, you must wait until it subsides.

Country in which there are precipitous cliffs with torrents running between, deep natural hollows, confined places, tangled thickets, quagmires and crevasses, should be left with all possible speed and not approached.

While we keep away from such places, we should get the enemy to approach them; while we face them, we should let the enemy have them on his rear.

If in the neighborhood of your camp there should be any hilly country, ponds surrounded by aquatic grass, hollow basins filled with reeds, or woods with thick undergrowth, they must be carefully routed out and searched; for these are places where men in ambush or insidious spies are likely to be lurking.

When the enemy is close at hand and remains quiet, he is relying on the natural strength of his position.

When he keeps aloof and tries to provoke a battle, he is anxious for the other side to advance.

If his place of encampment is easy of access, he is tendering a bait.

Movement amongst the trees of a forest shows that the enemy is advancing. The appearance of a number of screens in the midst of thick grass means that the enemy wants to make us suspicious.

The rising of birds in their flight is the sign of an ambush. Startled beasts indicate that a sudden attack is coming.

Humble words and increased preparations are signs that the enemy is about to advance. Violent language and driving forward as if to the attack are signs that he will retreat.

When the light chariots come out first and take up a position on the wings, it is a sign that the enemy is forming for battle.

Peace proposals unaccompanied by a sworn covenant indicate a plot.

When there is much running about and the soldiers fall into rank, it means that the critical moment has come.

When some are seen advancing and some retreating, it is a lure.

When the soldiers stand leaning on their spears, they are faint from want of food.

If those who are sent to draw water begin by drinking themselves, the army is suffering from thirst.

If the enemy sees an advantage to be gained and makes no effort to secure it, the soldiers are exhausted.

If birds gather on any spot, it is unoccupied. Clamor by night betokens nervousness.

If there is disturbance in the camp, the general's authority is weak. If the banners and flags are shifted about, sedition is afoot. If the officers are angry, it means that the men are weary.

When an army feeds its horses with grain and kills its cattle for food, and when the men do not hang their cooking-pots over the camp-fires, showing that they will not return to their tents, you may know that they are determined to fight to the death.*

The sight of men whispering together in small knots or speaking in subdued tones points to disaffection amongst the rank and file.

Too frequent rewards signify that the enemy is at the end of his resources; too many punishments betray a condition of dire distress.

To begin by bluster, but afterwards to take fright at the enemy's numbers, shows a supreme lack of intelligence.

When envoys are sent with compliments in their mouths, it is a sign that the enemy wishes for a truce.

---

* Men eat grain; horses eat grass. Hence, the slaying of cattle means a preparation for the end.—MH

If the enemy's troops march up angrily and remain facing ours for a long time without either joining battle or taking themselves off again, the situation is one that demands great vigilance and circumspection.

If our troops are no more in number than the enemy that is amply sufficient; it only means that no direct attack can be made. What we can do is simply to concentrate all our available strength, keep a close watch on the enemy, and obtain reinforcements.

He who exercises no forethought but makes light of his opponents is sure to be captured by them.

If soldiers are punished before they have grown attached to you, they will not prove submissive; and, unless submissive, then will be practically useless. If, when the soldiers have become attached to you, punishments are not enforced, they will still be useless.

Therefore soldiers must be treated in the first instance with humanity, but kept under control by means of iron discipline. This is a certain road to victory.

If in training soldiers commands are habitually enforced, the army will be well disciplined; if not, its discipline will be bad.

If a general shows confidence in his men but always insists on his orders being obeyed, the gain will be mutual.

Chapter X

Dangers and Opportunities

Now an army is exposed to six varying calamities, not arising from natural causes, but from faults for which the general is responsible. These are: (1) flight; (2) insubordination; (3) collapse; (4) ruin; (5) disorganization; (6) rout.

Other conditions being equal, if one force is hurled against another ten times its size, the result will be the flight of the former.

When the common soldiers are too strong and their officers too weak, the result is insubordination. When the officers are too strong and the common soldiers too weak, the result is collapse.

When the higher officers are angry and insubordinate, and on meeting the enemy give battle on their own account from a feeling of resentment, before the commander-in-chief can tell whether or not he is in a position to fight, the result is ruin.

When the general is weak and without authority; when his orders are not clear and distinct; when there are no fixed duties assigned to officers and men, and the ranks are formed in a slovenly haphazard manner, the result is utter disorganization.

When a general, unable to estimate the enemy's strength, allows an inferior force to engage a larger one, or hurls a weak detachment against a powerful one, and neglects to place picked soldiers in the front rank, the result must be rout.

These are six ways of courting defeat, which must be carefully noted by the general who has attained a responsible post.

The natural formation of the country is the soldier's best ally; but a power of estimating the adversary, of controlling the forces of victory, and of shrewdly calculating difficulties, dangers, and distances, constitutes the test of a great general.

He who knows these things, and in fighting puts his knowledge into practice, will win his battles. He who knows them not, nor practices them, will surely be defeated.

If fighting is sure to result in victory, then you must fight, even though the ruler forbid it; if fighting will not result in victory, then you must not fight, even at the ruler's bidding.

The general who advances without coveting fame and retreats without fearing disgrace, whose only thought is to protect his country and do good service for his sovereign, is the jewel of the kingdom.

Regard your soldiers as your children, and they will follow you into the deepest valleys; look upon them as your own beloved sons, and they will stand by you even unto death.

If, however, you are indulgent, but unable to make your authority felt; kind-hearted, but unable to enforce your commands; and incapable, moreover, of quelling disorder: then your soldiers must be likened to spoilt children; they are useless for any practical purpose.

If we know that our own men are in a condition to attack, but are unaware that the enemy is not open to attack, we have gone only halfway towards victory.

If we know that the enemy is open to attack, but are unaware that our own men are not in a condition to attack, we have gone only halfway towards victory.

If we know that the enemy is open to attack, and also know that our men are in a condition to attack, but are unaware that the nature of the ground makes fighting impracticable, we have still gone only halfway towards victory.

Hence the experienced soldier, once in motion, is never bewildered; once he has broken camp, he is never at a loss.

Hence the saying: If you know the enemy and know yourself, your victory will not stand in doubt; if you know Heaven and know Earth, you may make your victory complete.

If asked how to cope with a great army of the enemy in orderly array and on the point of marching to the attack, I should say: "Begin by seizing something which your opponent holds dear; then he will be amenable to your will."

Rapidity is the essence of war: take advantage of the enemy's unreadiness, make your way by unexpected routes, and attack unguarded spots.

The following are the principles to be observed by an invading force: The further you penetrate into a country, the greater will be the solidarity of your troops, and thus the defenders will not prevail against you.

Make forays in fertile country in order to supply your army with food.

Carefully study the wellbeing of your men, and do not overtax them. Concentrate your energy and hoard your strength. Keep your army continually on the move, and devise unfathomable plans.

Throw your soldiers into positions whence there is no escape, and they will prefer death to flight. If they will face death, there is nothing they may not achieve. Officers and men alike will put forth their uttermost strength.

Soldiers when in desperate straits lose the sense of fear. If there is no place of refuge, they will stand firm. If they are in hostile country, they will show a stubborn front. If there is no help for it, they will fight hard.

Thus, without waiting to be marshaled, the soldiers will be constantly on the alert; without waiting to be asked, they will do your will; without restrictions, they will be faithful; without giving orders, they can be trusted.

Prohibit the taking of omens, and do away with superstitious doubts. Then, until death itself comes, no calamity need be feared.

If our soldiers are not overburdened with money, it is not because they have a distaste for riches; if their lives are not unduly long, it is not because they are disinclined to longevity.

On the day they are ordered out to battle, your soldiers may weep. But let them once be brought to bay, and they will display great courage.

The principle on which to manage an army is to set up one standard of courage which all must reach.

How to make the best of both strong and weak—that is a question involving the proper use of ground.

Thus the skillful general conducts his army just as though he were leading a single man, in all places, by the hand.

It is the business of a general to be quiet and thus ensure secrecy; upright and just, and thus maintain order.

He must be able to mystify his officers and men by false reports and appearances, and thus keep them in total ignorance.

By altering his arrangements and changing his plans, he keeps the enemy without definite knowledge. By shifting his camp and taking circuitous routes, he prevents the enemy from anticipating his purpose.

At the critical moment, the leader of an army acts like one who has climbed up a height and then kicks away the ladder behind him. He carries his men deep into hostile territory before he shows his hand.

He burns his boats and breaks his cooking-pots;* like a shepherd driving a flock of sheep, he drives his men this way and that, and nothing knows whither he is going.

---

* The reference to burning boats and breaking cooking pots is akin to the Western expression to "burn the fleet"—in other words, to eliminate any way out and thus to guarantee victory or demise. This also makes a show of determination to troops and foes.—MH

To muster his army and bring it into danger—this may be termed the business of the general.

It is the soldier's disposition to offer an obstinate resistance when surrounded, to fight hard when he cannot help himself, and to obey promptly when he has fallen into danger.

We cannot enter into alliance with neighboring princes until we are acquainted with their designs. We are not fit to lead an army on the march unless we are familiar with the face of the country—its mountains and forests, its pitfalls and precipices, its marshes and swamps. We shall be unable to turn natural advantages to account unless we make use of local guides.

To be ignorant of any one of the following four or five principles does not befit a warlike prince.

When a warlike prince attacks a powerful state, his generalship shows itself in preventing the concentration of the enemy's forces. He overawes his opponents, and their allies are prevented from joining against him.

Hence he does not strive to ally himself with all and sundry, nor does he foster the power of other states. He carries out his own secret designs, keeping his antagonists in awe. Thus he is able to capture their cities and overthrow their kingdoms.

Bestow rewards without regard to rule, issue orders without regard to previous arrangements; and you will be able to handle a whole army as though you had to do with but a single man.

Confront your soldiers with the deed itself; never let them know your design. When the outlook is bright, bring it before their eyes; but tell them nothing when the situation is gloomy.*

Place your army in deadly peril, and it will survive; plunge it into desperate straits, and it will come off in safety.

For it is precisely when a force has fallen into harm's way that is capable of striking a blow for victory.

Success in warfare is gained by carefully accommodating ourselves to the enemy's purpose.

By persistently hanging on the enemy's flank, we shall succeed in the long run in killing the commander-in-chief.

This is called ability to accomplish a thing by sheer cunning.

If the enemy leaves a door open, you must rush in.

Forestall your opponent by seizing what he holds dear, and subtly contrive to time his arrival on the ground.

Walk in the path defined by rule, and accommodate yourself to the enemy until you can fight a decisive battle.

At first, then, exhibit the coyness of a maiden, until the enemy gives you an opening; afterwards emulate the rapidity of a running hare, and it will be too late for the enemy to oppose you.

Unhappy is the fate of one who tries to win his battles and succeed in his attacks without cultivating the spirit of

---

* In the first part of this principle, Sun Tzu is saying to focus troops on the goal not on the means to the goal.—MH

enterprise; for the result is waste of time and general stagnation.

Hence the saying: The enlightened ruler lays his plans well ahead; the good general cultivates his resources.

Move not unless you see an advantage; use not your troops unless there is something to be gained; fight not unless the position is critical.

No ruler should put troops into the field merely to gratify his own spleen; no general should fight a battle simply out of irritation.

If it is to your advantage, make a forward move; if not, stay where you are.

Anger may in time change to gladness; vexation may be succeeded by content.

But a kingdom that has once been destroyed can never come again into being; nor can the dead ever be brought back to life.

Hence the enlightened ruler is heedful, and the good general full of caution. This is the way to keep a country at peace and an army intact.

Chapter XI

The Use of Spies

Hostile armies may face each other for years, striving for the victory that is decided in a single day. This being so, to remain in ignorance of the enemy's condition simply because one grudges the outlay of a hundred ounces of silver in honors and payments is the height of inhumanity.

One who acts thus is no leader of men, no present help to his sovereign, no master of victory.

Thus, what enables the wise sovereign and the good general to strike and conquer, and achieve things beyond the reach of ordinary men, is foreknowledge.

Now this foreknowledge cannot be elicited from spirits; it cannot be obtained inductively from experience, nor by any deductive calculation.

Knowledge of the enemy's dispositions can only be obtained from other men.

Spies cannot be usefully employed without a certain intuitive sagacity.

They cannot be properly managed without benevolence and straightforwardness.

Without subtle ingenuity of mind, one cannot make certain of the truth of their reports.

Be subtle! be subtle! and use your spies for every kind of business.

Whether the object be to crush an army, to storm a city, or to assassinate an individual, it is always necessary to begin by finding out the names of the attendants, the aides-de-camp, and doorkeepers and sentries of the general in command. Our spies must be commissioned to ascertain these.

The enemy's spies who have come to spy on us must be sought out, tempted with bribes, led away, and comfortably housed. Thus they will become converted spies and available for our service.

About the Authors

Little is known about SUN TZU, who is estimated to have been born in 544 BC in the latter-era of China's Zhou dynasty, and died in 496 BC. Historians generally agree that Sun Tzu—an honorific title meaning "Master Sun"—was a commander in the dynastic army. His ancient treatise on strategy is one of the most widely read works of antiquity.

LIONEL GILES, whose groundbreaking 1910 translation of Sun Tzu is used in this abridgment, was a British sinologist and curator who also translated the works of Confucius and Lao Tzu. Born in 1875, he died in 1958.

POWER AND WEALTH

POWER AND WEALTH

*The Immortal Classics on
Will & Money—
Now in Special Condensations*

by Ralph Waldo Emerson

THE CONDENSED CLASSICS LIBRARY™

Contents

———•◆•———

Introduction

———

Genius and Practicality

by Mitch Horowitz

Part of Ralph Waldo Emerson's greatness as a writer is that he never shied away from practicality. This was true of his philosophical descendant William James, as well. It can be argued that Emerson's most practical works—which include his essays *Power* and *Wealth*—were not among his greatest. Critic Irving Howe wrote that in such works the philosopher "merely tugs the complexities . . . into the shallows of the explicit."

There is truth in this charge. And yet this judgment fails to take account of Emerson's bravery. Emerson felt obligated to be direct—to provide his readers with plans of action. If this approach reduced philosophical heights, it also banished authorial cowardice. Emerson would not dodge the question of *how* to practice the kinds of self-driven living that his philosophical essays endorsed.

Hence, it is in his essays *Power* and *Wealth*, which Emerson published in *The Conduct of Life* in 1860, that the Transcendentalist prescribed exactly how and under what conditions a person can successfully assert his will in outer life.

In *Power*, Emerson names four essential elements to exercising personal power. The first—and that which sustains all the others—is to be "in sympathy with the course of things." Displaying his innate instinct for Taoism and other Eastern philosophies, Emerson believed that an individual could read the *nature of things* and seek to merge with it, like a twig carried downstream. "The mind that is parallel with the laws of nature," he writes, "will be in the current of events, and strong with their strength."

The second element of power is *health*. Emerson means this on different levels. He is speaking broadly of the vitality of body and spirit; the state of physicality and personal morale that sustains risks, seeks adventure, and completes plans. But he also speaks of routine bodily health, without which the individual's energies are sapped.

The third element is *concentration*. One of nature's laws is that concentration of energies brings impact. The concentration of a striking blow delivers the greatest force. Too often we deplete our energies by dispersing or spreading thin our aims and efforts. In *Power,* an imaginary oracle says: "Enlarge not thy destiny, endeavor not to do more than is given thee in charge." Like light focused in a laser, concentration into a single beam brings the greatest power.

The fourth and final element of power is *drilling*. By this Emerson means repeating a practice over and over until you can perform it with excellence. The martial artist repeats his movements and routines to the point where they enter his physical memory and are available to him under all conditions. Likewise, we must drill—or practice or rehearse—to the point where we have mastered our chosen task.

In the essay *Wealth*, Emerson declares, chin out, that the individual is "born to be rich." And by riches, the philosopher is not employing a coy metaphor. He means cold, hard cash. But he also identifies accumulation of capital as befitting only that person who uses it to productive ends. Emerson writes,

> *Every man is a consumer, and ought to be a producer. He fails to make his place good in the world, unless he not only pays his debt, but also adds something to the common wealth. Nor can he do justice to his genius, without making some larger demand on the world than a bare subsistence. He is by constitution expensive, and needs to be rich.*

Only those purchases that expand your power and abilities, he writes, leave you any richer. Indeed, wealth that fails to accompany expansion is wealth thrown away. "Nor is the man enriched," Emerson writes, "in repeating the old experiments of animal sensation." Rather, you are enriched when you increase your ability to earn, to do, and to grow. Wealth, properly understood, is power. That is why these essays are conjoined.

So, how do you earn wealth? Emerson outlines roughly three steps: 1) First filling some nonnegotiable, subsistence-level need in your own life: this what drove the primeval farmers, hunter-gathers, and villagers. 2) Next, applying one's particular talents to nature, and expansively filling the needs of others. If you do not know or understand your talents, you must start there before anything is possible. Your particular talent is a source of excellence. And, finally, 3) using your wealth for the purposes of productiveness: paying down debts, making compound investments, and procuring the tools and talents of your trade. Building and expanding is the only sound way to riches. And such things also reflect your code and fiber as a progressing being.

By entering the mechanics of practicality, did Emerson sacrifice some of his transcendental splendor? Some thought so; I see it differently. If Emerson had avoided such an approach he would have been guilty of failing to take his philosophy onto the road. Complexity does not excuse inaction. And here I am reminded of an observation by the flawed and brilliant poet Ezra Pound, to whom I cede the last word: "But to have done instead of not doing/This is not vanity."

I. Power

Who shall set a limit to the influence of a human being? There are men, who, by their sympathetic attractions, carry nations with them, and lead the activity of the human race. And if there be such a tie, that, wherever the mind of man goes, nature will accompany him, perhaps there are men whose magnetisms are of that force to draw material and elemental powers, and, where they appear, immense instrumentalities organize around them. Life is a search after power; and this is an element with which the world is so saturated,—there is no chink or crevice in which it is not lodged,—that no honest seeking goes unrewarded. A man should prize events and possessions as the ore in which this fine mineral is found; and he can well afford to let events and possessions, and the breath of the body go, if their value has been added to him in the shape of power. If he have secured the elixir, he can spare the wide gardens from which it was distilled. A cultivated man, wise to know and bold to perform, is the end to which nature works, and the education of the will is the flowering and result of all this geology and astronomy.

All successful men have agreed in one thing,—they were *causationists*. They believed that things went not by luck, but by law; that there was not a weak or a cracked link in the chain that joins the first and last of things. A belief in causality, or strict connection between every trifle and the principle of being, and, in consequence, belief in compensation, or, that nothing is got for nothing,—characterizes all valuable minds, and must control every effort that is made by an industrious one. The most valiant men are the best believers in the tension of the laws. "All the great captains," said Bonaparte, "have performed vast achievements by conforming with the rules of the art,—by adjusting efforts to obstacles."

The key to the age may be this, or that, or the other, as the young orators describe—the key to all ages is—Imbecility; imbecility in the vast majority of men, at all times, and, even in heroes, in all but certain eminent moments; victims of gravity, custom, and fear. This gives force to the strong,—that the multitude have no habit of self-reliance or original action.

We must reckon success a constitutional trait. Courage—the old physicians taught, (and their meaning holds, if their physiology is a little mythical,)—courage, or the degree of life, is as the degree of circulation of the blood in the arteries. Where the arteries hold their blood, is courage and adventure possible. Where they pour it unrestrained into the veins, the spirit is low and feeble. For performance of great mark, it needs extraordinary health. If

Eric is in robust health, and has slept well, and is at the top of his condition, and thirty years old, at his departure from Greenland, he will steer west, and his ships will reach Newfoundland. But take out Eric, and put in a stronger and bolder man,—Biorn, or Thorfin,—and the ships will, with just as much ease, sail six hundred, one thousand, fifteen hundred miles further, and reach Labrador and New England. There is no chance in results. With adults, as with children, one class enter cordially into the game, and whirl with the whirling world; the others have cold hands, and remain bystanders; or are only dragged in by the humor and vivacity of those who can carry a dead weight. The first wealth is health. Sickness is poor-spirited, and cannot serve any one: it must husband its resources to live. But health or fullness answers its own ends, and has to spare, runs over, and inundates the neighborhoods and creeks of other men's necessities.

All power is of one kind, a sharing of the nature of the world. The mind that is parallel with the laws of nature will be in the current of events, and strong with their strength. One man is made of the same stuff of which events are made; is in sympathy with the course of things; can predict it. Whatever befalls, befalls him first; so that he is equal to whatever shall happen. A man who knows men, can talk well on politics, trade, law, war, religion. For, everywhere, men are led in the same manners.

The advantage of a strong pulse is not to be supplied by any labor, art, or concert. It is like the climate, which easily rears a crop, which no glass, or irrigation, or tillage, or manures, can elsewhere rival. It is like the opportunity of a city like New York, or Constantinople, which needs no diplomacy to force capital or genius or labor to it. They come of themselves, as the waters flow to it.

This affirmative force is in one, and is not in another, as one horse has the spring in him, and another in the whip. "On the neck of the young man," said Hafiz, "sparkles no gem so gracious as enterprise." Import into any stationary district, as into an old Dutch population in New York or Pennsylvania, or among the planters of Virginia, a colony of hardy Yankees, with seething brains, heads full of steam-hammer, pulley, crank, and toothed wheel,—and everything begins to shine with values. In every company, there is not only the active and passive sex, but, in both men and women, a deeper and more important *sex of mind*, namely, the inventive or creative class of both men and women, and the uninventive or accepting class. Each plus man represents his set, and, if he have the accidental advantage of personal ascendency,—which implies neither more nor less of talent, but merely the temperamental or taming eye of a soldier or a schoolmaster, (which one has, and one has not, as one has a black moustache and one a blond,) then quite easily and without envy or resistance, all his coadjutors and feeders will admit his right to absorb them.

There is always room for a man of force, and he makes room for many. Society is a troop of thinkers, and the best heads among them take the best places. A feeble man can see the farms that are fenced and tilled, the houses that are built. The strong man sees the possible houses and farms. His eye makes estates, as fast as the sun breeds clouds.

When a new boy comes into school, when a man travels, and encounters strangers every day, or, when into any old club a new comer is domesticated, that happens which befalls, when a strange ox is driven into a pen or pasture where cattle are kept; there is at once a trial of strength between the best pair of horns and the new comer, and it is settled thenceforth which is the leader. So now, there is a measuring of strength, very courteous, but decisive, and an acquiescence thenceforward when these two meet. Each reads his fate in the other's eyes. The weaker party finds, that none of his information or wit quite fits the occasion. He thought he knew this or that: he finds that he omitted to learn the end of it. Nothing that he knows will quite hit the mark, whilst all the rival's arrows are good, and well thrown. But if he knew all the facts in the encyclopaedia, it would not help him: for this is an affair of presence of mind, of attitude, of aplomb: the opponent has the sun and wind, and, in every cast, the choice of weapon and mark; and, when he himself is matched with some other antagonist, his own shafts fly well and hit. 'Tis a question of stomach and constitution. The second man is as good as the first,—perhaps better; but has not stoutness or stomach, as the first has, and so his wit seems over-fine or under-fine.

Health is good,—power, life, that resists disease, poison, and all enemies, and is conservative, as well as creative.

Vivacity, leadership, must be had, and we are not allowed to be nice in choosing. And we have a certain instinct, that where is great amount of life, though gross and peccant, it has its own checks and purifications, and will be found at last in harmony with moral laws.

We prosper with such vigor, that, like thrifty trees, which grow in spite of ice, lice, mice, and borers, so we do not suffer from the profligate swarms. The huge animals nourish huge parasites, and the rancor of the disease attests the strength of the constitution.

All kinds of power usually emerge at the same time; good energy, and bad; power of mind, with physical health; the ecstasies of devotion, with the exasperations of debauchery. The same elements are always present, only sometimes these conspicuous, and sometimes those; what was yesterday foreground, being to-day background—what was surface, playing now a not less effective part as basis. The longer the drought lasts, the more is the atmosphere surcharged with water. The faster the ball falls to the sun, the force to fly off is by so much augmented. And, in morals, wild liberty breeds iron conscience; natures with great impulses have great resources, and return from far. In politics, the sons of democrats will be whigs; whilst red republicanism, in the father, is a spasm of nature to engender an intolerable tyrant in the next age. On the other hand, conservatism, ever more timorous and narrow, disgusts the children, and drives them for a mouthful of fresh air into radicalism.

Those who have most of this coarse energy,—the 'bruisers,' who have run the gauntlet of caucus and tavern through the county or the state, have their own vices, but they have the good nature of strength and courage. Fierce and unscrupulous, they are usually frank and direct, and above falsehood. Our politics fall into bad hands, and churchmen and men of refinement, it seems agreed, are not fit persons to send to Congress. Politics is a deleterious profession, like some poisonous handicrafts. Men in power have no opinions, but may be had cheap for any opinion, for any purpose,—and if it be only a question between the most civil and the most forcible, I lean to the last.

In trade, also, this energy usually carries a trace of ferocity. Philanthropic and religious bodies do not commonly make their executive officers out of saints. The communities hitherto founded by Socialists,—the Jesuits, the Port-Royalists, the American communities at New Harmony, at Brook Farm, at Zoar, are only possible, by installing Judas as steward. The rest of the offices may be filled by good burgesses. The pious and charitable proprietor has a foreman not quite so pious and charitable. The most amiable of country gentlemen has a certain pleasure in the teeth of the bull-dog which guards his orchard. Of the Shaker society, it was formerly a sort of proverb in the country, that they always sent the devil to market. And in representations of the Deity, painting, poetry, and popular religion have ever drawn the wrath from Hell. It is an esoteric doctrine of society, that a little wickedness is good to make muscle; as if conscience were not good for hands and legs, as if poor decayed formalists of law and order cannot run like wild goats, wolves, and conies; that, as there is a use in medicine for poisons, so the world cannot move without rogues; that public spirit and the ready hand are as well found among the malignants. 'Tis not very rare, the coincidence of sharp private and political practice, with public spirit, and good neighborhood.

Whilst thus the energy for originating and executing work, deforms itself by excess, and so our axe chops off our own fingers,—this evil is not without remedy. All the elements whose aid man calls in, will sometimes become his masters, especially those of most subtle force. Shall he, then, renounce steam, fire, and electricity, or, shall he learn to deal with them? The rule for this whole class of agencies is,—all plus is good; only put it in the right place.

Men of this surcharge of arterial blood cannot live on nuts, herb-tea, and elegies; cannot read novels, and play whist; cannot satisfy all their wants at the Thursday Lecture, or the Boston Athenaeum. They pine for adventure, and must go to Pike's Peak; had rather die by the hatchet of a Pawnee, than sit all day and every day at a counting-room desk. They are made for war, for the sea, for mining, hunting, and clearing; for hair-breadth adventures, huge risks, and the joy of eventful living. Some men cannot endure an hour of calm at sea.

The excess of virility has the same importance in general history, as in private and industrial life. Strong race or strong individual rests at last on natural forces, which are best in the savage, who, like the beasts around him, is still in reception of the milk from the teats of Nature. Cut off the connection between any of our works, and this aboriginal source, and the work is shallow. The people lean on this, and the mob is not quite so bad an argument as we sometimes say, for it has this good side. "March without the people," said a French deputy from the tribune, "and you march into night: their instincts are a finger-pointing of Providence, always turned toward real benefit."

The best anecdotes of this force are to be had from savage life, in explorers, soldiers, and buccaneers. But who cares for fallings-out of assassins, and fights of bears, or grindings of icebergs? Physical force has no value, where there is nothing else. Snow in snow-banks, fire in volcanoes and solfataras is cheap. The luxury of ice is in tropical countries, and midsummer days. The luxury of fire is, to have a little on our hearth: and of electricity, not volleys of the charged cloud, but the manageable stream on the battery-wires.

In history, the great moment is, when the savage is just ceasing to be a savage, with all his hairy Pelasgic strength directed on his sense of beauty;—and you have Pericles and Phidias,—not yet passed over into the Corinthian civility. Everything good in nature and the world is in that moment of transition, when the swarthy juices still flow plentifully from nature, but their astringency or acridity is got out by ethics and humanity.

The triumphs of peace have been in some proximity to war. Whilst the hand was still familiar with the sword-hilt, whilst the habits of the camp were still visible in the port and complexion of the gentleman, his intellectual power culminated: the compression and tension of these stern conditions is a training for the finest and softest arts, and can rarely be compensated in tranquil times, except by some analogous vigor drawn from occupations as hardy as war.

We say that success is constitutional; depends on a *plus* condition of mind and body, on power of work, on courage; that it is of main efficacy in carrying on the world, and, though rarely found in the right state for an article of commerce, but oftener in the supersaturate or excess, which makes it dangerous and destructive, yet it cannot be spared, and must be had in that form, and absorbents provided to take off its edge.

The affirmative class monopolize the homage of mankind. They originate and execute all the great feats. What a force was coiled up in the skull of Napoleon! Of the sixty thousand men making his army at Eylau, it seems some thirty thousand were thieves and burglars. The men whom, in peaceful communities, we hold if we can, with iron at their legs, in prisons, under the muskets of sentinels, this man dealt with, hand to hand, dragged them to their duty, and won his victories by their bayonets.

This aboriginal might gives a surprising pleasure when it appears under conditions of supreme refinement, as in the proficients in high art. When Michel Angelo was forced to paint the Sistine Chapel in fresco, of which art he knew nothing, he went down into the Pope's gardens behind the Vatican, and with a shovel dug out ochres, red and yellow, mixed them with glue and water with his own hands, and having, after many trials, at last suited himself, climbed his ladders, and painted away, week after week, month after month, the sibyls and prophets. He surpassed his successors in rough vigor, as much as in purity of intellect and refinement. He was not crushed by his one picture left unfinished at last. Michel was wont to draw his figures first in skeleton, then to clothe them with flesh, and lastly to drape them. "Ah!" said a brave painter to me, thinking on these things, "if a man has failed, you will find he has dreamed instead of working. There is no way to success in our art, but to take off your coat, grind paint, and work like a digger on the railroad, all day and every day."

Success goes thus invariably with a certain *plus* or positive power: an ounce of power must balance an ounce of weight. And, though a man cannot return into his mother's womb, and be born with new amounts of vivacity, yet there are two economies, which are the best *succedanea* which the case admits. The first is, the stopping off decisively our miscellaneous activity, and concentrating our force on one or a few points; as the gardener, by severe pruning, forces the sap of the tree into one or two vigorous limbs, instead of suffering it to spindle into a sheaf of twigs.

"Enlarge not thy destiny," said the oracle: "endeavor not to do more than is given thee in charge." The one prudence in life is concentration; the one evil is dissipation: and it makes no difference whether our dissipations are coarse or fine; property and its cares, friends, and a social habit, or politics, or music, or feasting. Everything is good which takes away one plaything and delusion more, and drives us home to add one stroke of faithful work. Friends, books, pictures, lower duties, talents, flatteries, hopes,—all are distractions which cause oscillations in our giddy balloon, and make a good poise and a straight course impossible. You must elect your work; you shall take what your brain can, and drop all the rest. Only so, can that amount of vital force accumulate, which can make the step from knowing to doing. No matter how much faculty of idle seeing a man has, the step from knowing to doing is rarely taken. 'Tis a step out of a chalk circle of imbecility into fruitfulness. Many an artist lacking this, lacks all: he sees the masculine Angelo or Cellini with despair. He, too, is up to Nature and the First Cause in his thought. But the spasm to collect and swing his whole being into one act, he has not. The poet Campbell said, that "a man accustomed to work was equal to any achievement he resolved on, and, that, for himself, necessity not inspiration was the prompter of his muse."

Concentration is the secret of strength in politics, in war, in trade, in short, in all management of human affairs. One of the high anecdotes of the world is the reply of Newton to the inquiry, "how he had been able to achieve his discoveries?"—"By always intending my mind." Or if you will have a text from politics, take this from Plutarch: "There was, in the whole city, but one street in which Pericles was ever seen, the street which led to the market-place and the council house. He declined all invitations to banquets, and all gay assemblies and company. During the whole period of his administration, he never dined at the table of a friend." Or if we seek an example from trade,—"I hope," said a good man to Rothschild, "your children are not too fond of money and business: I am sure you would not wish that."—"I am sure I should wish that: I wish them to give mind, soul, heart, and body to business,—that is the way to be happy. It requires a great deal of boldness and a great deal of caution, to make a great fortune, and when you have got it, it requires ten times as much wit to keep it. If I were to listen to all the projects proposed to me, I should ruin myself very soon. Stick to one business, young man. Stick to your brewery, and you will be the great brewer of London. Be brewer, and banker, and merchant, and manufacturer, and you will soon be in the Gazette."

Many men are knowing, many are apprehensive and tenacious, but they do not rush to a decision. But in our flowing affairs a decision must be made,—the best, if you can; but any is better than none. There are twenty ways of going to a point, and one is the shortest; but set out at once on one. A man who has that presence of mind which can bring to him on the instant all he knows, is worth for action a dozen men who know as much, but can only bring it to light slowly. The good Speaker in the House is not the man who knows the theory of parliamentary tactics, but the man who decides off-hand. The good judge is not he who does hair-splitting justice to every allegation, but who, aiming at substantial justice, rules something intelligible for the guidance of suitors. The good lawyer is not the man who has an eye to every side and angle of contingency, and qualifies all his qualifications, but who throws himself on your part so heartily, that he can get you out of a scrape. Dr. Johnson said, in one of his flowing sentences, "Miserable beyond all names of wretchedness is that unhappy pair, who are doomed to reduce beforehand to the principles of abstract reason all the details of each domestic day. There are cases where little can be said, and much must be done."

The second substitute for temperament is drill, the power of use and routine. The hack is a better roadster than the Arab barb. In chemistry, the galvanic stream, slow, but continuous, is equal in power to the electric spark, and is, in our arts, a better agent. So in human action, against the spasm of energy, we offset the continuity of drill. We spread the same amount of force over much time, instead of condensing it into a moment. 'Tis the same ounce of gold here in a ball, and there in a leaf. At West Point, Col. Buford, the chief engineer, pounded with a hammer on the trunnions of a cannon, until he broke them off. He fired a piece of ordnance some hundred times in swift succession, until it burst. Now which stroke broke the trunnion? Every stroke. Which blast burst the piece? Every blast. The worst provincial company of actors would go through a

lime economies by which it may be attained. The world is mathematical, and has no casualty, in all its vast and flowing curve. Success has no more eccentricity, than the gingham and muslin we weave in our mills. I know no more affecting lesson to our busy, plotting New England brains, than to go into one of the factories with which we have lined all the watercourses in the States. A man hardly knows how much he is a machine, until he begins to make telegraph, loom, press, and locomotive, in his own image. But in these, he is forced to leave out his follies and hindrances, so that when we go to the mill, the machine is more moral than we. Let a man dare go to a loom, and see if he be equal to it. Let machine confront machine, and see how they come out. The world-mill is more complex than the calico-mill, and the architect stooped less. In the gingham-mill, a broken thread or a shred spoils the web through a piece of a hundred yards, and is traced back to the girl that wove it, and lessens her wages. The stockholder, on being shown this, rubs his hands with delight. Are you so cunning, Mr. Profitloss, and do you expect to swindle your master and employer, in the web you weave? A day is a more magnificent cloth than any muslin, the mechanism that makes it is infinitely cunninger, and you shall not conceal the sleezy, fraudulent, rotten hours you have slipped into the piece, nor fear that any honest thread, or straighter steel, or more inflexible shaft, will not testify in the web.

II. Wealth

As soon as a stranger is introduced into any company, one of the first questions which all wish to have answered, is, How does that man get his living? And with reason. He is no whole man until he knows how to earn a blameless livelihood. Society is barbarous, until every industrious man can get his living without dishonest customs.

Every man is a consumer, and ought to be a producer. He fails to make his place good in the world, unless he not only pays his debt, but also adds something to the common wealth. Nor can he do justice to his genius, without making some larger demand on the world than a bare subsistence. He is by constitution expensive, and needs to be rich.

Wealth has its source in applications of the mind to nature, from the rudest strokes of spade and axe, up to the last secrets of art. Intimate ties subsist between thought and all production; because a better order is equivalent to vast amounts of brute labor. The forces and the resistances are Nature's, but the mind acts in bringing things from where they abound to where they are wanted; in wise combining; in directing the practice of the useful arts, and in the creation of finer values, by fine art, by eloquence, by song, or the reproductions of memory. Wealth is in applications of mind to nature; and the art of getting rich consists not in industry, much less in saving, but in a better order, in timeliness, in being at the right spot. One man has stronger arms, or longer legs; another sees by the course of streams, and growth of markets, where land will be wanted, makes a clearing to the river, goes to sleep, wakes up rich. Steam is no stronger now, than it was a hundred years ago; but is put to better use. A clever fellow was acquainted with the expansive force of steam; he also saw the wealth of wheat and grass rotting in Michigan. Then he cunningly screws on the steam-pipe to the wheat-crop. Puff now, O Steam! The steam puffs and expands as before, but this time it is dragging all Michigan at its back to hungry New York and hungry England. Coal lay in ledges under the ground since the Flood, until a laborer with pick and windlass brings it to the surface. We may well call it black diamonds. Every basket is power and civilization. For coal is a portable climate. It carries the heat of the tropics to Labrador and the polar circle: and it is the means of transporting itself whithersoever it is wanted. Watt and Stephenson whispered in the ear of mankind their secret, that *a half-ounce of coal will draw two tons a mile*, and coal carries coal, by rail and by boat, to make Canada as warm as Calcutta, and with its comfort brings its industrial power.

When the farmer's peaches are taken from under the tree, and carried into town, they have a new look, and a hundredfold value over the fruit which grew on the same bough, and lies fulsomely on the ground. The craft of the merchant is this bringing a thing from where it abounds, to where it is costly.

Wealth begins in a tight roof that keeps the rain and wind out; in a good pump that yields you plenty of sweet water; in two suits of clothes, so to change your dress when you are wet; in dry sticks to burn; in a good double-wick lamp; and three meals; in a horse, or a locomotive, to cross the land; in a boat to cross the sea; in tools to work with; in books to read; and so, in giving, on all sides, by tools and auxiliaries, the greatest possible extension to our powers, as if it added feet, and hands, and eyes, and blood, length to the day, and knowledge, and good-will.

Wealth begins with these articles of necessity. And here we must recite the iron law which Nature thunders in these northern climates. First, she requires that each man should feed himself. If, happily, his fathers have left him no inheritance, he must go to work, and by making his wants less, or his gains more, he must draw himself out of that state of pain and insult in which she forces the beggar to lie. She gives him no rest until this is done: she starves, taunts, and torments him, takes away warmth, laughter, sleep, friends, and daylight, until he has fought his way to his own loaf. Then, less peremptorily, but still with sting enough, she urges him to the acquisition of such things as belong to him. Every warehouse and shop-window, every fruit-tree, every thought of every hour, opens a new want to him, which it concerns his power and dignity to gratify. It is of no use to argue the wants down: the philosophers have laid the greatness of man in making his wants few; but will a man content himself with a hut and a handful of dried pease? He is born to be rich. He is thoroughly related; and is tempted out by his appetites and fancies to the conquest of this and that piece of nature, until he finds his well-being in the use of his planet, and of more planets than his own. Wealth requires, besides the crust of bread and the roof,—the freedom of the city, the freedom of the earth, travelling, machinery, the benefits of science, music, and fine arts, the best culture, and the best company. He is the rich man who can avail himself of all men's faculties. He is the richest man who knows how to draw a benefit from the labors of the greatest number of men, of men in distant countries, and in past times. The same correspondence that is between thirst in the stomach, and water in the spring, exists between the whole of man and the whole of nature. The elements offer their service to him. The sea, washing the equator and the poles, offers its perilous aid, and the power and empire that follow it,—day by day to his craft and audacity. "Beware of me," it says, "but if you can hold me, I am the key to all the lands." Fire offers, on its side, an equal power. Fire, steam, lightning, gravity, ledges of rock, mines of iron, lead, quicksilver, tin, and gold; forests of all woods; fruits of all climates; animals of all habits; the powers of tillage; the fabrics of his chemic laboratory; the webs of his loom; the masculine draught of his locomotive, the talismans of the machine-shop; all grand and subtile things, minerals, gases, ethers, passions, war, trade, government, are his natural playmates, and, according to the excellence of the machinery in each human being, is his attraction for the instruments he is to employ. The world is his tool-chest, and he is successful, or his education is carried on just so far, as is the marriage of his faculties with nature, or, the degree in which he takes up things into himself.

The strong race is strong on these terms. The Saxons are the merchants of the world; now, for a thousand years, the leading race, and by nothing more than their quality of personal independence, and, in its special modification, pecuniary independence. No reliance for bread and games on the government, no clanship, no patriarchal style of living by the revenues of a chief, no marrying-on,—no system of clientship suits them; but every man must pay his scot. The English are prosperous and peaceable, with their habit of considering that every man must take care of himself, and has himself to thank, if he do not maintain and improve his position in society.

The subject of economy mixes itself with morals, inasmuch as it is a peremptory point of virtue that a man's independence be secured. Poverty demoralizes. A man in debt is so far a slave; and Wall-street thinks it easy for a millionaire to be a man of his word, a man of honor, but, that, in failing circumstances, no man can be relied on to keep his integrity. And when one observes in the hotels and palaces of our Atlantic capitals, the habit of expense, the riot of the senses, the absence of bonds, clanship, fellow-feeling of any kind, he feels, that, when a man or a woman is driven to the wall, the chances of integrity are frightfully diminished, as if virtue were coming to be a luxury which few could afford, or, as Burke said, "at a market almost too high for humanity." He may fix his inventory of necessities and of enjoyments on what scale he pleases, but if he wishes the power and privilege of thought, the chalking out his own career, and having society on his own terms, he must bring his wants within his proper power to satisfy.

The manly part is to do with might and main what you can do. The world is full of fops who never did anything, and who have persuaded beauties and men of genius to wear their fop livery, and these will deliver the fop opinion, that it is not respectable to be seen earning a living; that it is much more respectable to spend without earning; and this doctrine of the snake will come also from the elect sons of light; for wise men are not wise at all hours, and will speak five times from their taste or their humor, to once from their reason. The brave workman, who might betray his feeling of it in his manners, if he do not succumb in his practice, must replace the grace or elegance forfeited, by the merit of the work done. No matter whether he make shoes, or statues, or laws. It is the privilege of any human work which is well done to invest the doer with a certain haughtiness. He can well afford not to conciliate, whose faithful work will answer for him. The mechanic at his bench carries a quiet heart and assured manners, and deals on even terms with men of any condition. The artist has made his picture so true, that it disconcerts criticism. The statue is so beautiful, that it contracts no stain from the market, but makes the market a silent gallery for itself. The case of the young lawyer was pitiful to disgust,—a paltry matter of buttons or tweezer-cases; but the determined youth saw in it an aperture to insert his dangerous wedges, made the insignificance of the thing forgotten, and gave fame by his sense and energy to the name and affairs of the Tittleton snuffbox factory.

Society in large towns is babyish, and wealth is made a toy. The life of pleasure is so ostentatious, that a shallow observer must believe that this is the agreed best use of wealth, and, whatever is pretended, it ends in cosseting. But, if this were the main use of surplus capital, it would bring us to barricades, burned towns, and tomahawks, presently. Men of sense esteem wealth to be the assimilation of nature to themselves, the converting of the sap and juices of the planet to the incarnation and nutriment of their design. Power is what they want,—not candy;—power to execute their design, power to give legs and feet, form and actuality to their thought, which, to a clear-sighted man, appears the end for which the Universe exists, and all its resources might be well applied. Columbus thinks that the sphere is a problem for practical navigation, as well as for closet geometry, and looks on all kings and peoples as cowardly landsmen, until they dare fit him out. Few men on the planet have more truly belonged to it. But he was forced to leave much of his map blank. His successors inherited his map, and inherited his fury to complete it.

So the men of the mine, telegraph, mill, map, and survey,—the monomaniacs, who talk up their project in marts, and offices, and entreat men to subscribe:—how did our factories get built? how did North America get netted with iron rails, except by the importunity of these orators, who dragged all the prudent men in? Is party the madness of many for the gain of a few? This speculative genius is the madness of few for the gain of the world. The projectors are sacrificed, but the public is the gainer. Each of these idealists, working after his thought, would make it tyrannical, if he could. He is met and antagonized by other speculators, as hot as he. The equilibrium is preserved by these counteractions, as one tree keeps down another in the forest, that it may not absorb all the sap in the ground. And the supply in nature of railroad presidents, copper-miners, grand-junctioners, smoke-burners, fire-annihilators, etc., is limited by the same law which keeps the proportion in the supply of carbon, of alum, and of hydrogen.

To be rich is to have a ticket of admission to the master-works and chief men of each race. It is to have the sea, by voyaging; to visit the mountains, Niagara, the Nile, the desert, Rome, Paris, Constantinople; to see galleries, libraries, arsenals, manufactories. The reader of Humboldt's "Cosmos" follows the marches of a man whose eyes, ears, and mind are armed by all the science, arts, and implements which mankind have anywhere accumulated, and who is using these to add to the stock. So is it with Denon, Beckford, Belzoni, Wilkinson, Layard, Kane, Lepsius, and Livingston. "The rich man," says Saadi, "is everywhere expected and at home." The rich take up something more of the world into man's life. They include the country as well as the town, the ocean-side, the White Hills, the Far West, and the old European homesteads of man, in their notion of available material. The world is his, who has money to go over it. He arrives at the sea-shore, and a sumptuous ship has floored and carpeted for him the stormy Atlantic, and made it a luxurious hotel, amid the horrors of tempests. The Persians say, "'Tis the same to him who wears a shoe, as if the whole earth were covered with leather."

Kings are said to have long arms, but every man should have long arms, and should pluck his living, his instruments, his power, and his knowing, from the sun, moon, and stars. Is not then the demand to be rich legitimate? Yet, I have never seen a rich man. I have never seen a man as rich as all men ought to be, or, with an adequate command of nature. The pulpit and the press have many commonplaces denouncing the thirst for wealth; but if men should take these moralists at their word, and leave off aiming to be rich, the moralists would rush to rekindle at all hazards this love of power in the people, lest civilization should be undone. Men are urged by their ideas to acquire the command over nature. Ages derive a culture from the wealth of Roman Caesars, Leo Tenths, magnificent Kings of France, Grand Dukes of Tuscany, Dukes of Devonshire, Townleys, Vernons, and Peels, in England; or whatever great proprietors. It is the interest of all men, that there should be Vaticans and Louvres full of noble works of art; British Museums, and French Gardens of Plants, Philadelphia Academies of Natural History, Bodleian, Ambrosian, Royal, Congressional Libraries. It is the interest of all that there should be Exploring Expeditions; Captain Cooks to voyage round the world, Rosses, Franklins, Richardsons, and Kanes, to find the magnetic and the geographic poles. We are all richer for the measurement of a degree of latitude on the earth's surface. Our navigation is safer for the chart. How intimately our knowledge of the system of the Universe rests on that!—and a true economy in a state or an individual will forget its frugality in behalf of claims like these.

Whilst it is each man's interest, that, not only ease and convenience of living, but also wealth or surplus product should exist somewhere, it need not be in his hands. Often it is very undesirable to him. Goethe said well, "nobody should be rich but those who understand it." Some men are born to own, and can animate all their possessions. Others cannot: their owning is not graceful; seems to be a compromise of their character: they seem to steal their own dividends. They should own who can administer; not they who hoard and conceal; not they who, the greater proprietors they are, are only the greater beggars, but they whose work carves out work for more, opens a path for all. For he is the rich man in whom the people are rich, and he is the poor man in whom the people are poor: and how to give all access to the masterpieces of art and nature, is the problem of civilization. The socialism of our day has done good service in setting men on thinking how certain civilizing benefits, now only enjoyed by the opulent, can be enjoyed by all. For example, the providing to each man the means and apparatus of science, and of the arts. There are many articles good for occasional use, which few men are able to own. Every man wishes to see the ring of Saturn, the satellites and belts of Jupiter and Mars; the mountains and craters in the moon: yet how few can buy a telescope! and of those, scarcely one would like the trouble of keeping it in order, and exhibiting it. So of electrical and chemical apparatus, and many the like things. Every man may have occasion to consult books which he does not care to possess, such as cyclopaedias, dictionaries, tables, charts, maps, and public documents: pictures also of birds, beasts, fishes, shells, trees, flowers, whose names he desires to know.

There is a refining influence from the arts of Design on a prepared mind, which is as positive as that of music, and not to be supplied from any other source. But pictures, engravings, statues, and casts, beside their first cost, entail expenses, as of galleries and keepers for the exhibition; and the use which any man can make of them is rare, and their value, too, is much enhanced by the numbers of men who can share their enjoyment. In the Greek cities, it was reckoned profane, that any person should pretend a property in a work of art, which belonged to all who could behold it. I think sometimes,—could I only have music on my own terms;—could I live in a great city, and know where I could go whenever I wished the ablution and inundation of musical waves,—that were a bath and a medicine.

If properties of this kind were owned by states, towns, and lyceums, they would draw the bonds of neighborhood closer. A town would exist to an intellectual purpose. In Europe, where the feudal forms secure the permanence of wealth in certain families, those families buy and preserve these things, and lay them open to the public. But in America, where democratic institutions divide every estate into small portions, after a few years, the public should step into the place of these proprietors, and provide this culture and inspiration for the citizen.

Man was born to be rich, or, inevitably grows rich by the use of his faculties; by the union of thought with nature. Property is an intellectual production. The game requires coolness, right reasoning, promptness, and patience in the players. Cultivated labor drives out brute labor. An infinite number of shrewd men, in infinite years, have arrived at certain best and shortest ways of doing, and this accumulated skill in arts, cultures, harvestings, curings, manufactures, navigations, exchanges, constitutes the worth of our world to-day.

Commerce is a game of skill, which every man cannot play, which few men can play well. The right merchant is one who has the just average of faculties we call common sense; a man of a strong affinity for facts, who makes up his decision on what he has seen. He is thoroughly persuaded of the truths of arithmetic. There is always a reason, in the man, for his good or bad fortune, and so, in making money. Men talk as if there were some magic about this, and believe in magic, in all parts of life. He knows, that all goes on the old road, pound for pound, cent for cent,—for every effect a perfect cause,—and that good luck is another name for tenacity of purpose. He insures himself in every transaction, and likes small and sure gains. Probity and closeness to the facts are the basis, but the masters of the art add a certain long arithmetic. The problem is, to combine many and remote operations, with the accuracy and adherence to the facts, which is easy in near and small transactions; so to arrive at gigantic results, without any compromise of safety. Napoleon was fond of telling the story of the Marseilles banker, who said to his visitor, surprised at the contrast between the splendor of the banker's chateau and hospitality, and the meanness of the counting-room in which he had seen him,—"Young man, you are too young to understand how masses are formed,—the true and only power,—whether composed of money, water, or men, it is all alike,—a mass is an immense centre of motion, but it must be begun, it must be kept up:"—and he might have added, that the way in which it must be begun and kept up, is, by obedience to the law of particles.

Success consists in close appliance to the laws of the world, and, since those laws are intellectual and moral, an intellectual and moral obedience. Political Economy is as good a book wherein to read the life of man, and the ascendency of laws over all private and hostile influences, as any Bible which has come down to us.

Money is representative, and follows the nature and fortunes of the owner. The coin is a delicate meter of civil, social, and moral changes. The farmer is covetous of his dollar, and with reason. It is no waif to him. He knows how many strokes of labor it represents. His bones ache with the day's work that earned it. He knows how much land it represents;—how much rain, frost, and sunshine. He knows that, in the dollar, he gives you so much discretion and patience so much hoeing, and threshing. Try to lift his dollar; you must lift all that weight. In the city, where money follows the skit of a pen, or a lucky rise in exchange, it comes to be looked on as light. I wish the farmer held it dearer, and would spend it only for real bread; force for force.

The farmer's dollar is heavy, and the clerk's is light and nimble; leaps out of his pocket; jumps on to cards and faro-tables: but still more curious is its susceptibility to metaphysical changes. It is the finest barometer of social storms, and announces revolutions.

The value of a dollar is social, as it is created by society. Every man who removes into this city, with any purchasable talent or skill in him, gives to every man's labor in the city, a new worth. If a talent is anywhere born into the world, the community of nations is enriched; and, much more, with a new degree of probity. The expense of crime, one of the principal charges of every nation, is so far stopped. In Europe, crime is observed to increase or abate with the price of bread.

Wealth brings with it its own checks and balances. The basis of political economy is non-interference. The only safe rule is found in the self-adjusting meter of demand and supply. Do not legislate. Meddle, and you snap the sinews with your sumptuary laws. Give no bounties: make equal laws: secure life and property, and you need not give alms. Open the doors of opportunity to talent and virtue, and they will do themselves justice, and property will not be in bad hands. In a free and just commonwealth, property rushes from the idle and imbecile, to the industrious, brave, and persevering.

Our nature and genius force us to respect ends, whilst we use means. We must use the means, and yet, in our most accurate using, somehow screen and cloak them, as we can only give them any beauty, by a reflection of the glory of the end. That is the good head, which serves the end, and commands the means. The rabble are corrupted by their means: the means are too strong for them, and they desert their end.

1. The first of these measures is that each man's expense must proceed from his character. As long as your genius

buys, the investment is safe, though you spend like a monarch. Nature arms each man with some faculty which enables him to do easily some feat impossible to any other, and thus makes him necessary to society. This native determination guides his labor and his spending. He wants an equipment of means and tools proper to his talent. Do your work, respecting the excellence of the work, and not its acceptableness. Nothing is beneath you, if it is in the direction of your life: nothing is great or desirable, if it is off from that. I think we are entitled here to draw a straight line, and say, that society can never prosper, but must always be bankrupt, until every man does that which he was created to do.

Spend for your expense, and retrench the expense which is not yours. Allston, the painter, was wont to say, that he built a plain house, and filled it with plain furniture, because he would hold out no bribe to any to visit him, who had not similar tastes to his own. We are sympathetic, and, like children, want everything we see. But it is a large stride to independence,—when a man, in the discovery of his proper talent, has sunk the necessity for false expenses.

2. Spend after your genius, and by system. Nature goes by rule, not by sallies and saltations. There must be system in the economies. Saving and unexpensiveness will not keep the most pathetic family from ruin, nor will bigger incomes make free spending safe. The secret of success lies never

in the amount of money, but in the relation of income to outgo; as if, after expense has been fixed at a certain point, then new and steady rills of income, though never so small, being added, wealth begins.

3. The rule is not to dictate, nor to insist on carrying out each of your schemes by ignorant wilfulness, but to learn practically the secret spoken from all nature, that things themselves refuse to be mismanaged, and will show to the watchful their own law. Nobody need stir hand or foot. The custom of the country will do it all. I know not how to build or to plant; neither how to buy wood, nor what to do with the house-lot, the field, or the wood-lot, when bought. Never fear: it is all settled how it shall be, long beforehand, in the custom of the country, whether to sand, or whether to clay it, when to plough, and how to dress, whether to grass, or to corn; and you cannot help or hinder it. Nature has her own best mode of doing each thing, and she has somewhere told it plainly, if we will keep our eyes and ears open.

4. Another point of economy is to look for seed of the same kind as you sow: and not to hope to buy one kind with another kind. Friendship buys friendship; justice, justice; military merit, military success. Good husbandry finds wife, children, and household. The good merchant large gains, ships, stocks, and money. The good poet fame, and literary credit; but not either, the other. Yet there is com-

monly a confusion of expectations on these points. Hotspur lives for the moment; praises himself for it; and despises Furlong, that he does not. Hotspur, of course, is poor; and Furlong a good provider. The odd circumstance is, that Hotspur thinks it a superiority in himself, this improvidence, which ought to be rewarded with Furlong's lands.

5. Now these things are so in Nature. All things ascend, and the royal rule of economy is, that it should ascend also, or, whatever we do must always have a higher aim. Thus it is a maxim, that money is another kind of blood. So there is no maxim of the merchant, e.g., "Best use of money is to pay debts;" "Every business by itself;" "Best time is present time;" "The right investment is in tools of your trade;" or the like, which does not admit of an extended sense. The counting-room maxims liberally expounded are laws of the Universe. The merchant's economy is a coarse symbol of the soul's economy. It is, to spend for power, and not for pleasure. It is to invest income; that is to say, to take up particulars into generals; days into integral eras,—literary, emotive, practical, of its life, and still to ascend in its investment. The merchant has but one rule, absorb and invest: he is to be capitalist: the scraps and filings must be gathered back into the crucible; the gas and smoke must be burned, and earnings must not go to increase expense, but to capital again. Well, the man must be capitalist. Will he spend his income, or will he invest? His body and every organ is under the same law. His body is a jar, in which the

liquor of life is stored. Will he spend for pleasure? The way to ruin is short and facile. Will he not spend, but hoard for power? It passes through the sacred fermentations, by that law of Nature whereby everything climbs to higher platforms, and bodily vigor becomes mental and moral vigor. The bread he eats is first strength and animal spirits: it becomes, in higher laboratories, imagery and thought; and in still higher results, courage and endurance. This is the right compound interest; this is capital doubled, quadrupled, centupled; man raised to his highest power.

The true thrift is always to spend on the higher plane; to invest and invest, with keener avarice, that he may spend in spiritual creation, and not in augmenting animal existence. Nor is the man enriched, in repeating the old experiments of animal sensation, nor unless through new powers and ascending pleasures, he knows himself by the actual experience of higher good, to be already on the way to the highest.

About the Author

Born in 1803 in Boston, Massachusetts, RALPH WALDO EMERSON was one of America's preeminent men of letters. The inspiration for the school of philosophy called Transcendentalism, Emerson, in his essays, journals, lectures, and letters, traced out a view of life that located man as an extension and reflection of the Divine, owing his existence and allegiance to none but the highest insights of his own nature. An inspiration on figures ranging from his contemporary Henry David Thoreau to William James, Emerson formulated what can be called the American spiritual vision: non-dogmatic, nonsectarian, and based in the integrity and primacy of the individual spiritual search. In that sense, Emerson is also the founding figure of much of the modern spiritual culture in the West. After many years as a writer, publisher, lecturer, and seeker, he died in 1882 in Concord, Massachusetts, where his house still stands today.

Atom-Smashing
Power of Mind

ATOM-
SMASHING
POWER OF
MIND

*The Life-Changing Classic
on Your Power Within*

by Charles Fillmore

THE CONDENSED CLASSICS LIBRARY™

Contents

Introduction

——— ◆ ———

Charles Fillmore:
The Man Who Never Stood Still

by Mitch Horowitz

Spiritual experimenters through the ages, from ancient astrologers and alchemists to contemporary chaos magicians and mind-power mystics, have always availed themselves of the latest technologies of their eras. The New Thought pioneer Charles Fillmore, who founded the vibrant and ongoing Unity movement, was a great example of this.

Born in 1854 on an Indian reservation near St. Cloud, Minnesota, Fillmore and his wife and intellectual partner Myrtle, organized their Kansas City-based Unity ministry into one of the nation's first mass-media ministries. As early as 1907, the Fillmores staffed phone banks with round-the-clock volunteers ready to assist callers with distance prayers. The Unity ministry made early use of radio, targeted mailings, correspondence courses, pamphlets, and well-produced magazines aimed at the large demographic range of Unity's congregants. This included the children's monthly *Wee Wisdom*, which launched the literary career of bestselling novelist Sidney Sheldon when it published the ten-year-old's first poem in 1927.

Up to the eve of his death in 1948, Charles Fillmore remained well versed in the science and technology of the newly dawned atomic era. Fillmore sought to unite the insights of science and practical mysticism in the collection of writings that make up *Atom-Smashing Power of the Mind*, which appeared the year after his death.

This 1949 book is one of Fillmore's finest literary efforts. It serves as a powerful and stirring summation of his theology of mind-power metaphysics. At the same time, Fillmore relates the higher abilities of thought to the revolutions in atomic energy that entered public awareness in the years immediately preceding his death. Of this, Fillmore makes a creditable effort, foreseeing future developments in wireless, microwave, and cellular technology. When I consider my failings to stay fully versed in the digital technology of our own era, I am all the more admiring of a frontier boy who grew up not only to establish a major religious denomination but who never stopped learning about the radically changing world around him. Within those changes, Fillmore discovered confirmation of his own universal ideals.

This condensation of *Atom-Smashing Power of Mind* captures the verve, spirit, and soaring language of his original, while retaining his key points and practical insights.

I consider Fillmore's book one of the finest mid-century statements of New Thought philosophy. It is the kind of work that should inspire those of us today who believe that all knowledge—scientific, technological, psychological, medical, and spiritual—ultimately converge. Of this, Charles Fillmore was absolutely certain.

Chapter One

The Atomic Age

The majority of people have crude or distorted ideas about the character and the location of Spirit. They think that Spirit plays no part in mundane affairs and can be known by a person only after his death.

But Jesus said, "God is Spirit;" He also said, "The kingdom of God is within you." Science tells us that there is a universal life that animates and sustains all the forms and shapes of the universe. Science has broken into the atom and revealed it to be charged with tremendous energy that may be released and be made to give the inhabitants of the earth powers beyond expression when its law of expression is discovered.

Jesus evidently knew about this hidden energy in matter and used His knowledge to perform so-called miracles.

Our modern scientists say that a single drop of water contains enough latent energy to blow up a ten-story building. This energy, existence of which has been discovered by modern scientists, is the same kind of spiritual energy that was known to Elijah, Elisha, and Jesus, and used by them to perform miracles.

By the power of his thought Elijah penetrated the atoms and precipitated an abundance of rain. By the same law he increased the widow's oil and meal. This was not a miracle—that is, it was not a divine intervention supplanting natural law—but the exploitation of a law not ordinarily understood. Jesus used the same dynamic power of thought to break the bonds of the atoms composing the few loaves and fishes of a little lad's lunch—and five thousand people were fed.

Science is discovering the miracle-working dynamics of religion, but science has not yet comprehended the dynamic directive power of man's thought. All so-called miracle workers claim that they do not of themselves produce the marvelous results; that they are only the instruments of a superior entity. It is written in I Kings, "The jar of meal wasted not, neither did the cruse of oil fail, according to the word of Jehovah, which he spake by Elijah." Jesus called Jehovah Father. He said, "The works that I do in my Father's name, these bear witness of me."

Jesus did not claim to have the exclusive supernatural power that is usually credited to Him. He had explored the ether energy, which He called the "kingdom of the heavens;" His understanding was beyond that of the average man, but He knew that other men could do what He did if they would only try. He encouraged His followers to take Him as a center of faith and use the power of thought and word. "He that believeth on me, the works that I do shall he do also; and greater works than these shall he do."

Have faith in the power of your mind to penetrate and release the energy that is pent up in the atoms of your body, and you will be astounded at the response. Paralyzed functions anywhere in the body can be restored to action by one's speaking to the spiritual intelligence and life within them. Jesus raised His dead bodies in this way, and Paul says that we can raise our body in the same manner if we have the same spiritual contact.

What have thought concentration and discovery of the dynamic character of the atom to do with prayer? They have everything to do with prayer, because prayer is the opening of communication between the mind of man and the mind of God. Prayer is the exercise of faith in the presence and power of the unseen God. Supplication, faith, meditation, silence, concentration, are mental attitudes that enter into and form part of prayer. When one understands the spiritual character of God and adjusts himself mentally to the omnipresent God-Mind, he has begun to pray rightly.

Audible prayers are often answered but the most potent are silently uttered in the secret recesses of the soul. Jesus warned against wordy prayers—prayer uttered to be heard of men. He told His disciples not to be like those who pray on the housetop. "When thou prayest, enter into thine inner chamber, and having shut thy door, pray to thy Father who is in secret, and thy Father who seeth in secret shall recompense thee."

The times are ripe for great changes in our estimate of the abiding place and the character of God. The six-day creation of the universe (including man) described in Genesis is a symbolic story of the work of the higher realms of mind under divine law. It is the privilege of everyone to use his mind abilities in the superrealms, and thereby carry out the prayer formula of Jesus: "Seek ye first his kingdom, and his righteousness; and all these things shall be added unto you."

Of all the comments on or discussions of the indescribable power of the invisible force released by the atomic bomb none that we have seen mentions its spiritual or mental character. All commentators have written about it as a force external to man to be controlled by mechanical means, with no hint that it is the primal life that animates and interrelates man's mind and body.

The next great achievement of science will be the understanding of the mental and spiritual abilities latent in man through which to develop and release these tremendous electrons, protons, and neutrons secreted in the trillions of cells in the physical organism.

Here is involved the secret, as Paul says, "hid for ages and generations . . . which is Christ [superman] in you, the hope of glory." It is through release of these hidden life forces in his organism that man is to achieve immortal life, and in no other way. When we finally understand the facts of life and rid our minds of the delusion that we shall find immortal life after we die, then we shall seek more diligently to awaken the spiritual man within us and strengthen and build up the spiritual domain of our being until, like Jesus, we shall be able to control the atomic energy in our bodies and perform so-called miracles.

The fact is that all life is based upon the interaction between the various electrical units of the universe. Science tells us about these activities in terms of matter and no one understands them, because they are spiritual entities and their realities can only be understood and used wisely by the spiritually developed man. Electricians do not know what electricity is, although they use it constantly. The Christian uses faith and gets marvelous results, the electrician uses electricity and also gets marvelous results, and neither of them knows the real nature of the agent he uses so freely.

The man who called electricity faith doubtless thought that he was making a striking comparison when in fact he was telling a truth, that faith is of the mind and it is the match that starts the fire in the electrons and protons of innate Spirit forces. Faith has its degrees of voltage; the faith of the child and the faith of the most powerful spiritual adept are far apart in their intensity and results. When the trillions of cells in one's body are roused to expectancy by spiritual faith, a positive spiritual contact results and marvelous transformations take place.

Sir James Jeans, the eminent British scientist, gives a prophecy of this in one of his books. He says in substance that it may be that the gods determining our fate are our own minds working on our brain cells and through them on the world about us.

This will eventually be found to be true, and the discovery of the law of release of the electronic vitality wrapped up in matter will be the greatest revelation of all time.

When we awake to the fact that every breath we draw is releasing this all-potent electronic energy and it is shaping our lives for good or ill, according to our faith, then we shall begin to search for the law that will guide us aright in the use of power.

CHAPTER TWO

The Restorative Power of the Spirit

Not only our Bible but the scriptures of all the nations of the world testify to the existence of an invisible force moving men and nature in their various activities. Not all agree as to the character of this omnipresent force, universal Spirit, but it serves the purpose of being their god under whatever name it may appear. Different nations ostensibly believe in the same scriptures, but they have various concepts of the universal Spirit; some conceive it to be nature and others God. Robert Browning says, "What I call God . . . fools call Nature."

Our Bible plainly teaches that God implanted in man His perfect image and likeness, with executive ability to carry out all the creative plans of the Great Architect. When man arrives at a certain point in spiritual understanding it is his office to cooperate with the God principle in creation.

As the animating life of all things God is a unit, but as the mind that drives this life He is diverse. Every man is king in his own mental domain, and his subjects are his thoughts.

People in this atomic-age civilization ask why God does not reveal Himself now as He did in Bible days. The fact is that God is talking to people everywhere, but they do not understand the message and brush it aside as an idle dream. We need to divest ourselves of the thought that Daniel and Joseph, in fact all the unusually wise men of the Bible, were especially inspired by God, that they were divinely appointed by the Lord to do His work. Everything points to their spiritual insight as the result of work on their part to that end.

The body is the instrument of the mind, and the mind looks to the Spirit for its inspiration. Not only the Scriptures that we look to for authority in our daily living but also the experience of ourselves and our neighbors proves that those who cultivate communion with the Father within become conscious of a guiding light, call it what you will.

Those who scoff at this and say that it is all the work of the imagination are deluding themselves and ignoring a source of instruction and progress that they need above all things. If this sense world were the only world we shall ever know, the attainment of its ambitions might be sufficient for a man of meager outlook and small capacity, but the majority of us see ourselves and the world about us in a process of transformation that will culminate in conditions here on the earth far superior to those we have imagined for heaven.

Jesus was very advanced, and His radiant body was developed in larger degree than that of anyone in our race, but we all have this body, and its development is in proportion to our spiritual culture. In Jesus this body of light glowed "as he was praying." Jesus' body did not go down to corruption, but He, by the intensity of His spiritual devotion, restored every cell to its innate state of atomic light and power. When John was in the state of spiritual devotion Jesus appeared to him, "and his eyes were as a flame of fire; and his feet like unto burnished brass." Jesus lives today in that body of glorified electricity in a kingdom that interpenetrates the earth and its environment. He called it the kingdom of the heavens.

We do not have to look to the many experiences recorded in the Bible of the spiritually illumined to prove the existence of the spiritual supersubstance. People everywhere are discovering it, as they always have in every age and clime.

The metaphysical literature of our day is very rich with the experiences of those who have found through various channels the existence of the radiant body. This prompts me to tell of my development of the radiant body, during half a century's experience. It began when I was mentally affirming statements of Truth. Just between my eyes, but above, I felt a "thrill" that lasted a few moments, then passed away. I found I could repeat this experience with affirmations. As time went on I could set up this "thrill" at other points in my body and finally it became a continuous current throughout my nervous system. I called it "the Spirit" and found that it was connected with a universal life force whose source was the Christ. As taught in the Bible, we have through wrong thinking and living lost contact with the parent life. Jesus Christ incarnated in the flesh and thereby introduced us by His Word into the original Father life. He said, "If a man keep my word, he shall never taste of death." I have believed that and affirmed His words until they have become organized in my body. Sometimes when I make this claim of Christ life in the body I am asked if I expect to live always in this flesh. My answer is that I realize that the flesh is being broken down every day and its cells transformed into energy and life, and a new body is being formed of a very superior quality. That new body in Christ will be my future habitation.

I have found that the kingdom of God is within man and that we are wasting our time and defeating the work of the Spirit if we look for it anywhere else.

Chapter Three

Spiritual Obedience

Zeal is the great universal force that impels man to spring forward in a field of endeavor and accomplish the seemingly miraculous. It is the inward fire that urges man onward, regardless of the intellectual mind of caution and conversation.

Zeal should be tempered with wisdom. It is possible to be so zealously active on the intellectual plane that one's vitality is consumed and there is nothing left for spiritual growth. "Take time to be holy." Never neglect your soul. To grow spiritually you should exercise your zeal in spiritual ways.

Above all other Bible writers Paul emphasizes the importance of the mind in the transformation of character and body. In this respect he struck a note in religion that had been mute up to this time; that is, that spirit and mind are akin and that man is related to God through his thought. Paul sounds again and again in various forms this silent but very essential chord in the unity of God and man and man and his body.

When the scientific world investigates the so-called miracles of religion and discovers that they are being duplicated continually, the power of mind over matter will be heralded as of great importance to both religion and science.

Prayer gives spiritual poise to the ego, and it brings forth eternal life when spiritually linked with the Christ. "If a man keep my word, he shall never see death."

To one who gains even a meager quickening of the Spirit, Christianity ceases to be a theory; it becomes a demonstrable science of the mind.

We must not anticipate better social and economic conditions until we have better men and women to institute and sustain those conditions.

Jesus said that He was the bread and substance that came down from heaven. When will our civilization begin to realize and appropriate this mighty ocean of substance and life?

A finer civilization than now exists has been conceived by many from Plato in his "Republic" to Edward Bellamy in "Looking Backward." But a new and higher civilization will be developed only through the efforts of higher and finer types of men and women. Philosophers and seers have looked forward to a time when this earth would produce superior men and women, but save Jesus none has had the spiritual insight to declare, "Verily I say unto you, This generation shall not pass away, until all these things be accomplished."

"Behold, the man!" Jesus Christ is the type of a new race now forming in the earth. Those who incorporate into consciousness the Christ principles are its members.

The dominion that God gave to man in the beginning, as recorded in Genesis, is a dominion over spiritual ideas, which are represented in the allegory by material symbols.

Hence to exercise his dominion man must understand the metaphysical side of everything in existence.

Divine Mind is the one and only reality. When we incorporate the ideas that form Divine Mind into our mind and persevere in those ideas, a mighty strength wells up within us. Then we have a foundation for the spiritual body, the body not made with hands, eternal in the heavens. When the spiritual body is established in consciousness, its strength and power is transmitted to the visible body and to all the things that we touch in the world about us.

In the economy of the future man will not be a slave to money. Humanity's daily needs will be met in ways not now thought practical.

In the new economy we shall serve for the joy of serving, and prosperity will flow to us and through us in rippling streams of plenty. The supply and support that love and zeal set in motion are not yet largely used by man, but those who have tested this method are loud in their praise of its efficiency.

Chapter Four

I AM or Superconciousness

Superconciousness is the goal toward which humanity is working. Regardless of appearances there is an upward trend continually active throughout all creation. The superconsciousness is the realm of divine ideas. Its character is impersonal. It therefore has no personal ambitions; knows no condemnation; but is always pure, innocent, loving, and obedient to the call of God.

The superconsciousness has been perceived by the spiritually wise in every age, but they have not known how to externalize it and make it an abiding state of consciousness. Jesus accomplished this, and His method is worthy of our adoption, because as far as we know, it is the only method that has been successful. It is set forth in the New Testament, and whoever adopts the life of purity and love and power there exemplified in the experiences of Jesus of Nazareth will in due course attain the place that He attained.

Jesus acknowledged Himself to be the Son of God. Living in the superconsciousness calls for nothing less on our part than a definite recognition of ourselves as sons of God right here and now, regardless of appearances to the contrary. We know that we are sons of God; then why not acknowledge it and proceed to take possession of our God heirdom? That is what Jesus did in the face of the most adverse conditions. Conditions today are not so inertly material as they were in Jesus' time. People now know more about themselves and their relation to God. They are familiar with thought processes and how an idea held in mind will manifest itself in the body and in affairs; hence they take up this problem of spiritual realization under vastly more favorable conditions. An idea must work out just as surely as a mathematical problem, because it is under immutable law. The factors are all in our possession, and the method was demonstrated in one striking instance and is before us. By following the method of Jesus and doing day-by-day work that comes to us, we shall surely put on Christ as fully and completely as did Jesus of Nazareth.

The method by which Jesus evolved from sense consciousness to God consciousness was, first, the recognition of the spiritual selfhood and a constant affirmation of its supremacy and power. Jesus loved to make the highest statements: "I and the Father are one." "All authority hath been given unto me in heaven and on earth." He made these statements, so we know that at the time He was fully aware of their reality. Secondly, by the power of His word He penetrated deeper into omnipresence and tapped the deepest resources of His mind, whereby He released the light, life, and substance of Spirit, which enabled Him to get the realization that wholly united His consciousness with the Father Mind.

In the light of modern science the miracles of the Bible can be rationally explained as Mind acting in an omnipresent spiritual field, which is open to all men who develop spiritually. "Ye who have followed me, in the regeneration when the Son of man shall sit on the throne of his glory, ye also shall sit upon twelve thrones, judging the twelve tribes of Israel."

"He that overcometh, I will give to him to sit down with me in my throne."

Overcoming is a change of mind from error to Truth. The way of overcoming is first to place one's self by faith in the realization of Sonship, and second, to demonstrate it in every thought and act.

The Word is man's I AM. The Holy Spirit is the "outpouring" or activity of the living Word. The work of the Holy Spirit is the executive power of Father (mind) and Son (idea), carrying out the creative plan. It is through the help of the Holy Spirit that man overcomes. The Holy Spirit reveals, helps, and directs in this overcoming. "The Spirit searcheth all things, yea, the deep things of God." It finally leads man into the light.

Science rightly understood is of inestimable value to religion, and Christianity in order to become the world power that its founder envisioned, must stress the unfoldment of the spiritual mind in man in order that he may do the mighty works promised by Jesus.

When Jesus went up into the mount to pray He was transfigured before His apostles

Peter, James, and John. True prayer brings about an exalted radiation of energy, and when it is accompanied by faith, judgment, and love, the word of Truth bursts forth in a stream of light that, when held in mind, illumines, uplifts, and glorifies.

Jesus recognized Mind in everything and called it "Father." He knew that there is a faith center in each atom of so-called matter and that faith in man can move upon the faith center in so-called matter and can remove mountains.

Jesus taught that the realities of God are capable of expression here in this world and that man within himself has God capacity and power. Jesus was crucified because He claimed to be the Son of God. Yet the Scriptures, which the Pharisees worshiped, had this bold proclamation, which Jesus quoted to them from Psalms 82:

"I said, Ye are gods,
And all of you sons of the Most High."

The reports by His followers of what He taught clearly point to two subjects that He loved to discourse upon. The first was the Son of God: He was the Son of God. Secondly: We might all become as He was and demonstrate our dominion by following Him in the regeneration.

In order to follow Jesus in the regeneration we must become better acquainted with the various phases of mind and how they function in and through the body.

In spiritual understanding we know that all the forces in the body are directed by thought and that they work in a constructive or a destructive way, according to the character of the thought. Medicine, massage, and all the material means accomplish but incomplete, unsatisfactory, temporary results, because they work only from the outside and do not touch the inner springs that control the forces. The springs can only be touched by thought. There must be a unity between the mind of man and Divine Mind so that ideas and thoughts that work constructively unto eternal life may be quickened in the mind and organism of man.

We are told in John that the world could not contain the books that would be written if all the things that Jesus did were put into writing. But enough is given in the story of His life and in the writings of the apostles concerning Him to bear witness to that which is daily being revealed in this day of fulfillment. Those who are consecrated to Truth and fully resolved to follow Jesus all the way are spiritualizing the whole man, including the body, which is being redeemed from corruption. Those who are living as Jesus lived are becoming like Him. "God is not the God of the dead, but of the living." Resurrection takes place in people who are alive.

Chapter Five

The Day of Judgment

It is said we are to be judged after death according to deeds done in the body, which are kept on record like books that are balanced; and if the balance is found to be in our favor we go up, and if against us we go down. But if we are spiritual now—divine—this spiritual part has dominion, and we begin to exercise this dominion. The moment we catch sight of this we begin to judge. We begin to put the thoughts that are good on the right and the others on the left. All our ideas of the attributes of our divine self we put on the right hand of power, while the thoughts of disease, death, limitation and lack we put on the left—denied, cut off.

This is not to occur after death. It is to begin right now!

Now is the time to plant the seed thought of the conditions we desire by saying, "Come my good thoughts, let us inherit our kingdom."

We do not fear anything, for we have separated our sheep from our goats; we have set our true thoughts on the right and have denied our error thoughts any power whatever.

Come into the kingdom of mind. Here everything that is in Principle is yours.

Everything, all good, is to be gathered up, and everything is good at its center. The essence of your body is good and of true substance. When you sift your consciousness of all but the real and true, the body becomes full of light.

The diamond owes its brilliance to the perfect arrangement of the innumerable little prisms within it, each of which refracts the light of the other. Man's body is made up of centers of consciousness—of light—and if arranged so they radiate the light within you, you will shine like the diamond. All things are in the consciousness and you have to learn to separate the erroneous from the true, darkness from light. The I AM must separate the sheep from the goats. This sifting begins right now and goes on until the perfect child of God is manifest and you are fully rounded out in all your Godlike attributes

Chapter Six

Thou Shalt Decree a Thing

To decree with assurance is to establish and fix an ideal in substance. The force behind the decree is invisible, like a promise to be fulfilled at a future time; but it binds with its invisible chains the one who makes it. We have only a slight conception of the strength of the intangible. We compare and measure strength by some strong element in nature. We say "strong as steel." But a very little thought will convince us that mental affirmations are far stronger than the strongest visible thing in the world. The reason for this is that visible things lack livingness. They are not linked with energy and intelligence as are words. Words charged with power and intelligence increase with use, while material things decrease.

It is not necessary to call the attention of metaphysicians to the fact that all visible things had their origin in the invisible. The visible is what remains of an idea that has gradually lost its energy. Scientists say that this so-called solid earth under our feet was once radiant substance. Nothing is really "solid" but the atomic energy latent in everything. They tell us that it takes some six billion years for uranium to disintegrate and become lead, and this rate of disintegration has helped scientists determine the age of the earth as about two billion years.

Since nothing is lost in the many transformations that occur in nature, what becomes of the energy that is being released in the disintegration that is going on in our earth? The answer is that a new earth is being formed in which matter will be replaced by atomic energy. This process of refining matter into radiant substance is taking place not only in the natural world but in our bodies also. In fact the speed with which the transformation takes place depends on the character of the thoughts that we project into our brains and through them into our bodies and the world about us. This is why we should spiritualize our thoughts and refine the food we eat to correspond.

At the present writing there is a housing shortage everywhere and the lack of materials and competent labor indicate that several years will elapse before the need is met. This is counted a calamity; but is it? The inventive genius of man is planning houses of glass and other materials that will be much less expensive—more durable and in every respect superior to the present homes. When man gets his ingenious mind into action he always meets every emergency with something better. Every adverse situation can be used as a spur to urge one to greater exertion and the ultimate attainment of some ideal that has lain dormant in the subconsciousness.

Chapter Seven

Thinking in the Fourth Dimension

Scientists tell us that the discoveries that their efforts are revealing convince them that they are just on the verge of stupendous truths. Christianity spiritually interpreted shows that Jesus understood the deeper things of God's universe. He understood exactly what the conditions were on the invisible side of life, which is termed in His teaching the "kingdom of God" or the "kingdom of the heavens." We are trying to connect His teaching with modern science in order to show the parallel; but as He said in Mark 4:23, "if any man hath ears to hear, let him hear." This means that we must develop a capacity for understanding in terms of the atomic structure of the universe.

Unless we have this spiritual capacity we do not understand. We think we have ears, but they are attuned to materiality. They do not get the radiations from the supermind, the Christ Mind. Physiology working with psychology is demonstrating that hearing and seeing can be developed in every cell in the body, independent of ears and eyes. We hear and see with our minds working through our bodies. This being true, the capacity to hear may extend beyond the physical ear into the spiritual ethers, and we should be able to hear the voice of God.

This extension of hearing is what Jesus taught. "If any man hath ears to hear, let him hear."

Then we are told that we must "take heed" what we hear. Many of us have found that as we develop this inner, spiritual hearing, we hear voices sometimes that do not tell the truth. These deceptive voices can be hushed by affirming the presence and power of the Lord Jesus Christ.

As you unfold your spiritual nature, you will find that it has the same capacity for receiving vibrations of sound as your outer, physical ear has. You do not give attention to all that you hear in the external; you discriminate as you listen. So in the development of this inner, spiritual ear take heed what you hear: discriminate.

Jesus said, "For he that hath, to him shall be given: and he that hath not, from him shall be taken away even that which he hath." How can what a man has not be taken away? We believe in our mortal consciousness that we have attained a great deal, but if we have not this inner, spiritual consciousness of reality our possessions are impermanent. Then we must be careful what we accumulate in our consciousness, because "he that hath, to him shall be given." The more spiritual Truth you pile up in your mind, the more you have of reality, and the larger is your capacity for the unlimited; but if you have nothing of a spiritual character, what little you have of intellectual attainment will eventually be taken away from you.

The mysteries of the supermind have always been considered the property of certain schools of occultists and mystics who were cautious about giving their truths to the masses for fear that in their ignorance these might misuse them. But now the doors are thrown wide open, and whosoever will may enter in.

Our attention in this day is being largely called to the revolution that is taking place in the economic world, but a revolution of even greater worth is taking place in the mental and spiritual worlds. A large and growing school of metaphysicians has made its advent in this generation, and it is radically changing the public mind toward religion. In other words, we are developing spiritual understanding, and this means that religion and its sources in tradition and in man are being inquired into and its principles applied in the development of a new cosmic mind for the whole human family.

CHAPTER EIGHT

Is This God's World?

W hy doesn't God do something about it?" This oft-repeated query, uttered by the skeptical and unbelieving, is heard day in and day out. Imitating the skeptics, Christian believers everywhere are looking to God for all kinds of reforms in every department of manifest life and also are charging Him with death and destruction the world over.

One who thinks logically and according to sound reason wonders at the contradictions set up by these various queries and desires.

Is God responsible for all that occurs on this earth, and if not all, how much of it?

The Bible states that God created the earth and all its creatures, and last of all man, to whom He gave dominion over everything. Observation and experience prove that man is gaining dominion over nature wherever he applies himself to that end. But so much remains to be gained, and he is so small physically that man counts himself a pygmy instead of the mental giant that he is.

All the real mastery that man attains in the world has its roots in his mind, and when he opens up the mental realm in his being there are no unattainables. If the conquests of the air achieved in the last quarter century had been prophesied, the prophets would have been pronounced crazy. The fact is that no one thinking in the old mind realm can have any conception of the transformation of sound waves into electromagnetic waves and back again into words and messages of intelligence. Edison admitted that his discovery of the phonograph was an accident and that he never fully understood how mechanical vibrations could be recorded and be reproduced in all forms of intelligent communication.

Now that man has broken away from his limited visualizations and mentally grasped the unhampered ideas of the supermind, he is growing grandly bold and his technical pioneers are telling him that the achievements of yesterday are as nothing compared to those of tomorrow. For example, an article by Harland Manchester condensed in the *Reader's Digest* from *Scientific American* tells of the "microwaves" that are slated for a more spectacular career in the realm of the unbelievable than anything that has preceded them. This article describes in detail some of the marvels that will evolve out of the utilization of microwaves, among which may be mentioned "private phone calls by the hundreds of thousands sent simultaneously over the same wave band without wires, poles or cables. Towns where each citizen has his own radio frequency, over which he can get voice, music, and television, and call any phone in the country by dialing. Complete abolition of static and interference from electrical devices and from other stations. A hundred times as much 'space on the air' as we now have in the commercial radio band. A high-definition and color television network to cover the country. And, perhaps most important of all, a nationwide radar network, geared to television, to regulate all air traffic and furnish instantaneous visual weather reports to airfields throughout the land."

Add to this the marvels promised by the appliers of atomic energy and you have an array of miracles unequaled in all the bibles of all the nations of the world.

It is admitted by those who are most familiar with the dynamic power of these newly discovered forces that we do not yet know how to protect our body cells from the destructiveness of their vibrations. Very thick concrete walls are required to protect those who experiment with atomic forces. One scientist says that the forces released from the bombs that were used on the Japanese cities in 1945 may affect those who were subjected to them and their descendants for a thousand years. Experimentation proves that we have tapped a kingdom that we do not know how to handle safely.

Chapter Nine

Truth Radiates Light

Spiritual light transcends in glory all the laws of matter and intellect. Even Moses could not enter the Tabernacle when it was aglow with this transcendent light.

It is written that the Israelites did not go forward on days when the cloud remained over the Tabernacle, but when the cloud was taken up they went forward. This means that there is no soul progress for man when his body is under the shadow of a "clouded" mind, but when the cloud is removed there is an upward and forward movement of the whole consciousness (all the people).

We are warned of the effect of thoughts that are against or opposed to the commandments of Jehovah. When we murmur and complain we cloud our minds, and Divine Mind cannot reach us or help us. Then we usually loaf until something turns up that causes us to think on happier things, when we go forward again.

Instead of giving up to circumstances and outer events we should remember that we are all very close to a kingdom of mind that would make us always happy and successful if we would cultivate it and make it and its laws a vital part of our life. "The joy of Jehovah is your strength."

You ask, "How can I feel the joy of Jehovah when I am poor, or sick, or unhappy?"

Jesus said, "Come unto me, all ye that labor and are heavy laden, and I will give you rest."

Here is the first step in getting out of the mental cloud that obscures the light of Spirit. Take the promises of Jesus as literally and spiritually true. Right in the midst of the most desperate situation one can proclaim the presence and power of Christ, and that is the first mental move in dissolving the darkness. You cannot think of Jesus without a feeling of freedom and light. Jesus taught freedom from mortality and proclaimed His glory so persistently that He energized our thought atmosphere into light.

The Scriptures state that when Moses came down from Mount Sinai with the Ten Commandments his face shone so brilliantly that the Children of Israel and even Aaron, his own brother, were afraid to come near him until he put a veil over his face. The original Hebrew says his face sent forth beams or horns of light.

The Vulgate says that Moses had "a horned face;" which Michelangelo took literally, in his statue of Moses representing him with a pair of horns projecting from the head. Thus we see the ludicrous effect of reading the Bible according to the letter.

Our men of science have experimented with the brain in action, and they tell us that it is true that we radiate beams when we think. The force of these beams has been measured.

Here we have further confirmation of the many statements in the Bible that have been taken as ridiculous and unbelievable or as miracles.

Persons who spend much time in prayer and meditate a great deal on spiritual things develop the same type of face that Moses is said to have had. We say of them that their faces fairly shine when they talk about God and His love. John saw Jesus on the island of Patmos, and he says, "His countenance was as the sun shineth in his strength."

I have witnessed this radiance in the faces of Truth teachers hundreds of times. I well remember one class lesson during which the teacher became so eloquent that beams of light shot forth from her head and tongues of fire flashed through the room, very like those which were witnessed when the followers of Jesus were gathered in Jerusalem.

We now know that fervent words expressed in prayer and song and eloquent proclamations of spiritual Truth release the millions of electrons in our brain cells and through them blend like chords of mental music with the Mind universal.

This tendency on our part to analyze and scientifically dissect the many supposed miracles recorded in the Bible is often regarded as sacrilegious, or at least as making commonplaces of some of the very spectacular incidents recorded in Scripture.

In every age preceding this the priesthood has labored under the delusion that the common people could not understand the real meaning of life and that they should therefore be kept in ignorance of its inner sources; also that the masses could not be trusted with sacred truths, that imparting such truths to them was like casting pearls before swine.

But now science is delving into hidden things, and it is found that they all arise in and are sustained by universal principles that are open to all men who seek to know and apply them.

Anyone who will search for the science in religion and the religion in science will find that they harmonize and prove each other. The point of unity is the Spirit-mind common to both. So long as religion assumes that the Spirit that creates and sustains man and the universe can be cajoled and by prayer or some other appeal can be induced to change its laws, it cannot hope to be recognized by those who know that unchangeable law rules everywhere and in everything.

Again, so long as science ignores the principle of intelligence in the evolutionary and directive forces of man and the universe, just so long will it fail to understand religion and the power of thought in the changes that are constantly taking place in the world, visible and invisible.

Chapter Ten

The Only Mind

I say, "An idea comes to me." Where did it come from? It must have had a source of like character with its own. Ideas are not visible to the eye, they are not heard by the ear, nor felt, nor tasted, yet we talk about them as having existence. We recognize that they live, move, and have being in the realm that we term mind.

This realm of mind is accepted by everybody as in some way connected with the things that appear, but because it is not describable in terms of length, breadth, and thickness, it is usually passed over as something too vague for consideration.

But those who take up the study of this thing called mind find that it can be analyzed and its laws and modes of operation understood.

To be ignorant of mind and its laws is to be a child playing with fire, or a man manipulating powerful chemicals without knowing their relation to one another. This is universally true; and all who are not learning about mind are in like danger, because all are dealing with the great cause from which spring forth all the conditions that appear in the lives of all men and women. Mind is the one reservoir from which we draw all that we make up into our world, and it is through the laws of mind that we form our lives. Hence nothing is as important as a knowledge of mind, its inherencies, and the mode of their expression.

The belief that mind cannot be understood is fallacious. Man is the expression of mind, dwells in mind, and can know more clearly and definitely about the mind than the things that appear in the phenomenal world.

Mind is the great storehouse of good from which man draws all his supplies. If you manifest life, you are confident that it had a source. If you show forth intelligence you know that somewhere in the economy of Being there is a fount of intelligence. So you may go over the elements that go to make up your being and you will find that they draw their sustenance from an invisible and, to your limited understanding, incomprehensible source.

This source we term Mind, because it is as such that our comprehension is best related to it. Names are arbitrary, and we should not stop to note differences that are merely technical. We want to get at the substance which they represent.

So if we call this invisible source Mind it is because it is of like character with the thing within our consciousness that we call our mind. Mind is manyfold in its manifestations. It produces all that appears. Not that the character of all that appears is to be laid to the volition of Mind; no, but some of its factors enter into everything that appears. This is why it is so important to know about Mind, and how its potentialities are made manifest.

And this is where we have set up a study that makes of every atom in the universe a living center of wisdom as well as life and substance.

We claim that on its plane of comprehension man may ask the atom or the mountain the secret that it holds and it will be revealed to him. This is the communication of mind with Mind; hence we call Mind the universal underlying cause of existence and study it from that basis.

God is Mind, and man made in the image and likeness of God is Mind, because there is but one Mind, and that is the Mind of God. The person in sense consciousness thinks he has a mind of his own and that he creates thought from its own inherent substance. This is a suppositional mind that passes away when the one and only real Mind is revealed. This one and only Mind of God that we study is the only creator. It is that which originates all that is permanent; hence it is the source of all reality. Its creations are of a character hard for the sense man to comprehend, because his consciousness is cast in a mold of space and time. These are changeable and transient, while the creations of the one Mind are substantial and lasting. But it is man's privilege to understand the creations of the one Mind, for it is through them that he makes his world. The creations of the one Mind are ideas. The ideas of God are potential forces waiting to be set in motion through proper formative vehicles. The thinking faculty in man is such a vehicle, and it is through this that the visible universe has existence. Man does not "create" anything if by this term is meant the producing of something from nothing; but he does make the formless up into form; or rather it is through his conscious cooperation that the one Mind forms its universe.

Mind is the storehouse of ideas. Man draws all his ideas from this omnipresent storehouse. The ideas of God, heaven, hell, devils, angels, and all things have their clue in Mind. But their form in the consciousness depends entirely upon the plane from which man draws his mental images. If he gets a "clue" to the character of God and then proceeds to clothe this clue idea with images from without, he makes God a mortal. If he looks within for the clothing of his clue idea he knows God to be the omnipresent Spirit of existence.

So it is of the utmost importance that we know how we have produced this state of existence which we call life; and we should be swift to conform to the only method calculated to bring harmony and success into our life, namely to think in harmony with the understanding derived from communion with the God-Mind.

CHAPTER ELEVEN

The Body

You see at once that man is not body, but that the body is the declaration of man, the substantial expression of his mind. We see so many different types of men that we are bound to admit that the body is merely the individual's specific interpretation of himself, whatever it may be. Man is an unknown quantity; we see merely the various ideas of man expressed in terms of body, but not man himself. The identification of man is determined by the individual himself, and he expresses his conception of man in his body.

Some persons have tall bodies; some have short ones. Some have fat bodies; some have slim ones. Some have distorted bodies, some have symmetrical ones. Now, if the body is the man, as claimed by sense consciousness, which of these many bodies is man?

The Bible declares that man is made in the "image" and after the "likeness" of God. Which of the various bodies just enumerated is the image and likeness of God?

Let us repeat that the body of man is the visible record of his thoughts. It is the individual's interpretation of his identity, and each individual shows in his body just what his views of man are. The body is the corporeal record of the mind of its owner, and there is no limit to its infinite differentiation. The individual may become any type of being that he elects to be. Man selects the mental model and the body images it. So the body is the image and likeness of the individual's idea of man. We may embody any conception of life or being that we can conceive. The body is the exact reproduction of the thoughts of its occupant. As a man thinks in his mind so is his body.

You can be an Adam if you choose, or you can be a Christ or any other type of being that you see fit to ideate. The choice lies with you. The body merely executes the mandates of the mind. The mind dictates the model according to which the body shall be manifested. Therefore as man "thinketh within himself [in his vital nature], so is he." Each individual is just what he believes he is.

It is safe to say that nine hundred and ninety-nine persons out of every thousand believe that the resurrection of the body has something specifically to do with the getting of a new body after death; so we find more than ninety-nine per cent of the world's population waiting for death to get something new in the way of a body. This belief is not based on the principles of Truth, for there is no ready-made-body factory in the universe, and thus none will get the body that he expects. Waiting for death in order to get a new body is the folly of ignorance. The thing to do is to improve the bodies that we now have; it can be done, and those who would follow Jesus in the regeneration must do it.

The "resurrection" of the body has nothing whatever to do with death, except that we may resurrect ourselves from every dead condition into which sense ignorance has plunged us. To be resurrected means to get out of the place that you are in and to get into another place. Resurrection is a rising into new vigor, new prosperity; a restoration to some higher state. It is absurd to suppose that it applies only to the resuscitation of a dead body.

It is the privilege of the individual to express any type of body that he sees fit to ideate. Man may become a Christ in mind and in body by incorporating into his every thought the ideas given to the world by Jesus.

Divine mind has placed in the mind of everyone an image of the perfect-man body. The imaging process in the mind may well be illustrated by the picture that is made by light on the photographic plate, which must be "developed" before it becomes visible. Or man's invisible body may be compared to the blueprint of a building that the architect delivers to the builder. Man is a builder of flesh and blood. Jesus was a carpenter. Also He was indeed the master mason. He restored the Lord's body ("the temple of Jehovah") in His mind and heart (in Jerusalem).

The resurrection of the body is not dependent for its demonstration on time, evolution, or any of the man-made means of growth. It is the result of the elevation of the spiritually emancipated mind of the individual.

Step by step, thought added to thought, spiritual emotion added to spiritual emotion—eventually the transformation is complete. It does not come in a day, but every high impulse, every pure thought, every upward desire adds to the exaltation and gradual personification of the divine in man and to the transformation of the human. The "old man" is constantly brought into subjection, and his deeds forever put off, as the "new man" appears arrayed in the vestments of divine consciousness.

How to accomplish the resurrection of the body has been the great stumbling block of man. The resurrection has been a mere hope, and we have endeavored to reconcile a dying body with a living God, but have not succeeded. No amount of Christian submission or stoical philosophy will take away the sting of death. But over him who is risen in Christ "death no more hath dominion."

CHAPTER TWELVE

Faith Precipitations

When asked what electricity is, a scientist replied that he had often thought of it as an adjunct to faith, judging from the way it acts. This linking of faith and electricity seems at first glance fantastic, but when we observe what takes place when certain substances in solution and an electric current are brought in conjunction, there seems to be a confirmation of the Scripture passage: "Now faith is assurance of things hoped for."

Just as the electric current precipitates certain metals in solution in acid, so faith stirs into action the electrons of man's brain; and acting concurrently with the spiritual ethers, these electrons hasten nature and produce quickly what ordinarily requires months of seedtime and harvest.

Speedy answers to prayer have always been experienced and always will be when the right relations are established between the mind of the one who prays and the spiritual realm, which is like an electrical field. The power to perform what seems to be miracles has been relegated to some God-selected one; but now we are inquiring into the law, since God is no respecter of persons, and we find that the fulfillment of the law rests with man or a group of men, when they quicken by faith the spiritual forces latent within them.

The reason why some prayers are not answered is lack of proper adjustment of the mind of the one who prays to the omnipresent creative spiritual life.

Jesus was the most successful demonstrator of prayer of whom we have any record, and He urged persistence in prayer. If at first you don't succeed, try, try again. Like Lincoln, Jesus loved to tell stories to illustrate His point, and He emphasized the value of persistence in prayer. He told of a woman who demanded justice of a certain judge and importuned him until in sheer desperation he granted her request.

Every Christian healer has had experiences where persistent prayer saved his patient. If he had merely said one prayer, as if giving a prescription for the Lord to fill, he would have fallen far short of demonstrating the law. Elijah prayed persistently until the little cloud appeared or, as we should say, he had a "realization;" then the manifestation followed.

Chapter Thirteen

The End of the Age

I n all ages and among all people, there have been legends of prophets and saviors and predictions of their coming.

The fact that all who believe in the principle of divine incarnation have long strained their eyes across the shining sands in an effort to catch sight of the coming of one clothed with the power of heaven, should make us pause and consider the cause of such universality of opinion among peoples widely separated. To dismiss the subject as a religious superstition is not in harmony with unprejudiced reason. To regard these prophecies merely as religious superstitions rules out traditions that are as tenable and as reliable as the facts of history. There is a cause for every effect, and the cause underlying this almost unanimous expectation of a messiah must have some of the omnipresence of a universal law.

In considering a subject like this, which demonstrates itself largely on metaphysical lines, it is necessary to look beyond the material plane to the realm of causes.

The material universe is but the shadow of the spiritual universe. The pulsations of the spiritual forces impinge upon and sway men, nations, and planets, according to laws whose sweep in space and time is so stupendous as to be beyond the ken or comprehension of astronomy. But the fact should not be overlooked that higher astronomy had its votaries in the past. The Magi and the illumined sages of Chaldea and Egypt had astronomical knowledge of universal scope. It was so broad, so gigantic, so far removed from the comprehension of the common mind of their day that it always remained the property of the few. It was communicated in symbols, because of the poverty of language to express its supermundane truths. In the sacred literature of the Hindus are evidences of astronomical erudition covering such vast periods of time that modern philosophers cannot or do not give them credence, and they are relegated to the domain of speculation rather than of science. However the astronomers of the present age have forged along on material lines until now they are beginning to impinge upon the hidden wisdom of the mighty savants of the past.

There is evidence that proves that the ages of the distant past knew a higher astronomy than do we of this age, and that they predicted the future of this planet through cycles and aeons—its nights of mental darkness and the dawn of its spiritual day—with the same accuracy that our astronomers do its present-day planetary revolutions.

Jesus evidently understood the aeons or ages through which earth passes. For example, in Matthew 13:39, our English Bible reads: "The enemy that sowed them is the devil: and the harvest is the end of the world; and the reapers are angels." In the Diaglott version, which gives the original

Greek and a word-for-word translation, this reads: "THAT ENEMY who SOWED them is the ADVERSARY; the HARVEST is the End of the Age; and the REAPERS are Messengers." In this as in many other passages where Jesus used the word "age," it has been translated "world," leading the reader to believe that Jesus taught that this planet was to be destroyed.

So we see that the almost universally accepted teaching of the end of the world is not properly founded on the Bible. The translators wanted to give the wicked a great scare, so they put "the end of the world" into Jesus' mouth in several instances where He plainly said "the end of the age."

The Bible is a textbook of absolute Truth; but its teachings are veiled in symbol and understood only by the illumined.

In accordance with the prophecies of the ancients, our planetary system has just completed a journey of 2,169 years, in which there has been wonderful material progress without its spiritual counterpart. But old conditions have passed away and a new era has dawned. A great change is taking place in the mentality of the race, and this change is evidenced in literature, science, and religion. There is a breaking away from old creeds and old doctrines, and there is a tendency to form centers along lines of scientific spiritual thought. The literature of the first half of the twentieth century is so saturated with occultism as to be an object of censure by conservatives, who denounce it as a "lapse into the superstition of the past." Notwithstanding the protests of the conservatives, on every hand are evidences of spiritual freedom; it crops out in so many ways that an enumeration would cover the whole field of life.

It is evident that Jesus and His predecessors had knowledge of coming events on lines of such absolute accuracy as to place it in the realm of truth ascertained, that is, exact science.

Do you belong to the old, or are you building anew from within and keeping time with the progress of the age? The "harvest" or "consummation of the age" pointed out by Jesus is not far off. This is no theological scare; it is a statement based on a law that is now being tested and proved.

Listen to your inner voice; cultivate the good, the pure, the God within you. Do not let your false beliefs keep you in the darkness of error until you go out like a dying ember. The divine spark is within you. Fan it into flame by right thinking, right living, and right doing, and you will find the "new Jerusalem."

About the Author

One of the pioneering leaders of the New Thought movement, CHARLES FILLMORE (1884–1948), with his wife Myrtle, founded the worldwide Unity ministry. An early visionary in using mass media to spread religious and inspirational messages, Fillmore was widely known for his metaphysical interpretations of the Bible, and for his books including *Prosperity*; *Christian Healing*; *Talks on Truth*; *Atom-Smashing Power of Mind*; and *The Twelve Powers*.

THE
MILLION DOLLAR
SECRET HIDDEN
IN YOUR MIND

THE
MILLION DOLLAR
SECRET HIDDEN
IN YOUR MIND

by Anthony Norvell

*The Lost Classic on
How to Control Your Thoughts
for Wealth, Power, and Mastery*

Abridged and Introduced
by Mitch Horowitz

THE CONDENSED CLASSICS LIBRARY™

Contents

———

Introduction

———◆·◆———

A Better Path to Power

by Mitch Horowitz

Y ou may have noticed a lot of books on attaining power making the rounds lately. Many of them, in my view, are unappealing. They encourage the pursuit of success without nobility, proffering methods like taking credit for other people's efforts or ideas, intimidating acquaintances, withholding information, and being a general sneak.

There is a better way. And it appears in the condensation you are about to experience of an overlooked and underestimated work from 1963: *The Million Dollar Secret Hidden in Your Mind.* Its author, Anthony Norvell, was a jack-of-all-trades success guru who reached his highest watermark with this practical, shrewd, and principled book. In it, Norvell makes memorable and substantive points about the non-exploitative pursuit of worldly success.

Norvell wrote with more edge than a Dale Carnegie, but always with an eye on legitimate personal growth. For example, Norvell pushes you to cultivate influence through the "law of proximity," which means seeking the company of people who encourage your finest traits, provide good examples to emulate or imitate, do not indulge your lowest habits, and challenge you to match them in mental acumen, not in money. Norvell observed how the most retrograde influences in your life are likely to come from "old neighborhood" friends and acquaintances, who forever see you as you were in childhood, and who nudge you toward past, and often dysfunctional, patterns of behavior.

Here are some of my favorite Norvell aphorisms. They may seem elementary but their meaning is deeper than may first appear.

- "Most people have a tendency to minimize themselves and their abilities."
- "To be great, you must dwell in the company of great thoughts and high ideals."
- "Do not be afraid to ask important people to help you."
- "Your subconscious mind will give you valuable ideas, but if you do not write them down, they leave suddenly, and it is difficult to recall them again."
- "Your mind likes *definiteness*. Give yourself a five-year plan for study, growth, and evolvement."
- "You must create a need in your life for the things you want."

- "Determine that you will never use your money for any destructive or degrading act."
- "*Know what you want of life.*"
- "You build your sense of self-importance by studying constantly."

Yes, there are more sophisticated works of mental therapeutics than Anthony Norvell's. You can read the essays of Ralph Waldo Emerson and William James (and you should); you can approach the complex metaphysics of Mary Baker Eddy and Thomas Troward; or you can immerse yourself in the luminous spiritual visions of Neville Goddard and Ernest Holmes. But there exists in Norvell's work a sapling of all those figures. What's more, Norvell writes with a delightful, infectious simplicity.

I often think of how to reply when asked to recommend a single book on mind power. This could be such a book. It is easily digestible and surprisingly broad in scope. You'll enjoy its ideas—but, above all, you must use them. Proof of their depth is in application.

CHAPTER ONE

Dynamic Thinkers Rule the World

A legend is told of the time when the Gods created man and the universe. They held a conference and one of them said, "Let us give man the same creative power that we ourselves possess. Where shall we hide this priceless gift?"

Another answered, "Let us hide it where man will never think to look for it; within his own mind."

And this is where the Million Dollar Secret resides; within your own mind, your own consciousness. Here it is that you can find all the creative power you will ever need to make a fortune or to give yourself a million dollars worth of health, happiness, friendship, love, and enjoyment in life.

The great philosopher Descartes had a philosophy that can be summarized in one dynamic sentence: "I think, therefore I am."

Dynamic thinking can set into motion a series of reactions that are cataclysmic in their effects.

Ask yourself: "What do I think?" Then answer candidly.

Do you think of yourself as a failure in life?

Do you think you are inferior and inadequate?

Do you think you are doomed to poverty all your life?

Do you think your personality is unattractive?

If you are thinking these negative thoughts, you are short-circuiting the dynamic power of your brain and creating the image of these negative conditions in the outer circumstances of your life. Thoughts are a psychological reality. We each live in a world colored and dominated by our own private thought atmosphere.

Change the picture of your thoughts from negative to positive. Dynamic thinking will cause you to **be** that which you **think**.

Think you are successful.

Think that you are adequate, that you are equal to others.

Think that you can achieve the riches that others have.

Think that your personality may become magnetic and attractive.

You are using the magical power of dynamic thinking in the moment that you think in a positive manner. "I think, therefore I am." Write that down on a card, which you can consult several times daily, and on that card also write, "I think and talk success, health, happiness, and achievement. I think great thoughts, therefore I am great."

Chapter Two

The Undiscovered Genius
Within Your Mind

There is a popular expression:

Sow a thought, reap a habit;
Sow a habit, reap a character;
Sow a character, reap a destiny.

Actually you build your future destiny thought by thought, and as these thoughts become more dynamic and perfect, they begin to shape your character and destiny in paths of greatness.

Now you are embarked upon the thrilling voyage of discovery that will lead you to the finding of new worlds, but there are shoals and pitfalls which I must warn you about.

Most of the pitfalls are your own relatives and friends. They have lived with you for many years and have been used to the shrinking violet you may have become under the regime of weak, negative thinking of the past. These friends and relatives feel comfortable in the presence of the small ego that fits their concept of your totality of power. When the slumbering mental giant that is within your mind begins to stir restlessly and tries to shake off the chains that bind it to mediocrity, failure, poverty, and ignorance, these people are apt to set up a clamor that will shock the giant back into his somnolent state of immobility and inertia.

Just remember that every genius of history has had to go through discouragement, often from people close to him, before breaking the bonds of negativity and frustration. A prophet is without honor in his own country, Scripture tells us. Those closest to you are sometimes the very last ones to recognize the genius within you or to give you recognition for having great talent.

Use these three steps to release the undiscovered genius within your mind:

1. Each day try to originate some new and daring concept of thought in relation to your life. Write these down in a notebook and begin to apply them to your activities.
2. Live in your imagination at least one half hour a day. See yourself as the person you wish to be. Visualize yourself as the manager of the department where you work See yourself owning your own business. Imagine yourself taking trips to foreign countries. Build the new concept of your great powers by seeing how many refinements you can make on inventions and technologies. Write down ideas for great stories, novels, movies. You may not intend to be a writer but this mental exercise will extend your thinking to the realm of creative

ideas and cause the subconscious mind to release more power to your everyday activities.

3. Pick some outstanding genius of history each day and emulate his philosophy, his thinking, his inspiration. Study the lives of great geniuses of history, searching for great thoughts which you may make a part of your own mental equipment. For instance, Pasteur. Concentrate on his persistence and patience. Edison. Borrow his vision and curiosity, and apply those qualities to your own life, seeing how many things you can mentally create, and how many useful facts you can discover.

Chapter Three

You Are Greater Than You Think

Most people have a tendency to minimize themselves and their abilities. Such people depreciate their own talents, their personalities, and tend to put others on a pedestal.

You cannot achieve a great destiny or a big fortune if you constantly believe yourself inferior and unworthy. Some people have subconscious feelings of guilt, put into their minds by their parents when they were children, and these guilt feelings hound them throughout life, making them unhappy, and dooming them to live lives that are inferior and inadequate. You may have been told that it is wrong and sinful to want to be successful, famous, and rich, and that only the "Meek shall inherit the earth." You must break such negativity at once, and believe *that you are greater than you think*.

The natural intelligence is greater in you than it is in all of nature's other creatures, for you represent the highest form of creation in the universe. When you discover the unlimited realm of the mind you can use it to shape the world you desire. This inner intuitive power that is in every animal, insect, bird and beast, is awaiting your recognition and bidding. When you once discover this power and learn through this study how to channel it correctly, you will be able to achieve seeming miracles in your own life.

Begin today to realize that you live in an unlimited universe, with unlimited resources. There are billions of worlds in outer space and science is now beginning to realize that more worlds are being born every day. The secret power back of all creation is intelligence.

To be great you must dwell in the company of great thoughts and high ideals. Your mind becomes stronger and more intelligent when you pass through it great thoughts, when you desire great things in your life, when you strive for high achievements. To expand your thinking into an area of importance and success, there must be a corresponding degree of inspiration and energy-drive in your thinking. If the idea held in consciousness is big enough, all the actions that follow will be of a like quality and degree.

It takes no more energy mentally to think of a big job, with good pay, than it does to think of an inferior position with small pay. People will set the value on you and your talents that you set on yourself.

All great men who have ever achieved anything worthwhile or enduring, have been infused with this higher purpose in living. There must be a change in your mental concept first; the idea that you want to express, the work you want to do, the home you want to live in; when you once **know for sure** what it is you want, and you hold tenaciously to that idea, your circumstances of life will gradually begin to change. Do not worry about how this higher mind within you is going to produce the change. You cannot tell this infinite intelligence, which rules the world, how to create an oak tree; this is God's secret. But you can plant the tiny acorn in the soil and then, under the universal laws of growth and capillary attraction, that acorn will attract to itself all the nourishment it needs from the soil and rain, to make a giant oak tree a hundred feet tall.

Do these things to become greater:

1. Build your sum of knowledge. You grow in mental power as your fund of knowledge grows.

2. Learn to crawl before you walk, but try to run as quickly as you gain strength and confidence in your power to walk. In other words, do not remain in a position that is inferior.

3. Make decisions quickly. Do not vacillate after making a decision, but act on your decision promptly.

4. Write to important people presenting your great ideas. Some people have won promotion and success through this process of calling attention to themselves.

5. Do not be afraid to ask important people to help you. They are human and are often flattered to think that you believe they are important enough to give you assistance.

CHAPTER FOUR

Tap the Hidden Treasures Within Your Mind

You may not think your ideas are valuable because they came from your brain. Change your attitude about the value of your thoughts. Some of the greatest things in the world were accomplished by men and women like you, who had just one good idea and made it pay dividends.

When I was lecturing in Honolulu, I met a man at my lectures who had invented the silent mercury switch for electric lights. He had been awakened so many times by the noise of the electric switch when his wife would turn it on at night that his mind began to think of some way to make the turning on of a light switch silent.

Your own ideas may be worth a fortune. You must sit quietly in your own room for at least half-an-hour daily and probe the goldmine of your mind. You should then write down all new ideas that come to you for improving your life, perfecting some product, marketing some merchandise you have created.

Start with whatever field you are in now, and do not wait for some better time or more improved conditions. Look around you, see what could be changed or improved, and then set about doing it. Start this process now and continue it the rest of your life, and you will see amazing results.

Epictetus said, "No great thing is created suddenly, any more than a bunch of grapes or a fig. If you tell me that you desire a fig, I answer you that there must be time. Let it first blossom, then bear fruit, then ripen."

Use this daily regimen for tapping the hidden treasures of your mind:

1. Begin each day, when you waken in the morning, by passing through your mind a series of big ideas relating to your life, your work, your environment. Ask yourself: "What can I do today to improve my situation in life? How can I improve my business? What ideas can I incorporate in my work that will pay me rich dividends in the future?"

2. Check your mind and see if you are using all the power that you possess or if you are wasting it on petty, unimportant things. Could you use more daring, courage, patience, persistence, thrift, sociability, optimism, humor in your relations with others? Are you using the gifts and talents you possess as steppingstones to greatness? Are you using the knowledge you possess fully? Do you seek the aid of important people you've met to help you achieve your goals?

3. Keep a daily diary in which you jot down each night the outstanding ideas you had during that day. Let your imagination soar without restraint, and carefully

note the ideas and suggestions that flash into your mind. Then write them down for future use. Many times your subconscious mind will give you valuable ideas, but if you do not write them down they leave suddenly and it is difficult to recall them again. Edison kept a notebook by his bedside, and his biggest ideas for his many inventions came to him while he slept. He wrote them down at once, and the next day acted on these inspirational ideas.

4. Stir your mind to action by holding in your mind each day a desire to achieve something important and worthwhile. An artist cannot paint his picture until he first has the visual image in his mind. The desire to create that particular picture stirs him into action and he projects his mental picture onto the canvas before him. You must do the same thing: hold in your mind daily the pictures of the things you wish to achieve. Do not worry how you will attain them. The law of cause and effect takes over the moment you have a strong idea in mind.

Chapter Five

Magnetism, the Law of Universal Attraction

You can magnetize what you want in life. You must image it mentally; clearly and emotionally, feeling it is already yours. You must write it down. You must visualize the persons, conditions, money, success—whatever it is you want clearly and as often as possible. The process known as daydreaming is helpful in fixing the image clearly in your mind. Daydream yourself in the situations in life you desire, such as singing, speaking or acting. Do the entire performance as if you were actually before that audience. Picture yourself in the job you desire, seeing yourself as an executive, giving orders, having other employees under you. Follow this process based on whatever desires you hold.

Energy and matter are interchangeable. The energy of the mind can be converted into material substance. For instance, the idea to build a bridge is only mental energy, but it can become externalized in the building of the actual bridge. The idea for a painting, a literary work, an invention, or a business is just as real and has a dimension that is as solid and actual as matter. The *idea for a thing* has inherent in it the ability to magnetize the thing itself and bring it into being. This is the way that your mental energy has in itself the equivalent of the thing you are holding in your mind. Be sure then that you magnetize *only* positive things.

The Bible speaks of it as, "As ye sow, so shall ye reap." This is the great mental law of attraction at work in nature.

Take these six steps for greater magnetic power:

1. Picture clearly the things that you want to magnetize and attract. Sit quietly in your room and run these pictures through your mind like film through a movie projector. Review these pictures daily, as often as possible, especially at night just before going to sleep. See them clearly; do *not* keep changing them, but have the pictures the same each time. Have as many things as you want to magnetize, taking them up one at a time, and giving about ten minutes to picturing each thought.

2. Write down the things you wish to magnetize. Write them clearly and briefly. This serves to imprint them on your subconscious more forcibly.

3. Engage in constructive daydreaming when possible. The moments you spend waiting for a car or bus, the time you take out for coffee or a break at work—use these precious moments to daydream. In these daydreams, see yourself as your ideal.

4. *Do not tell anyone* of the secret power you are using. They will tend to laugh at you, discourage you, and they may short-circuit your magnetic attraction with their negative ideas. The acorn grows in the secret, hid-

den womb of the earth, safe from all interference, and becomes an oak tree because of this secrecy. What if someone tore it up by the roots every few days to see if it was growing? It would die. So, too, your dreams die if they are shattered by others.

5. Have faith in the invisible intelligence that resides in nature to produce the things you are trying to magnetize. The secret power that can make a baby in nine months knows how to release the energy to bring your idea or dream to fruition. But you must have faith in this invisible power that creates all life.

6. Share your good with the world. There is magnetism in giving to others.

CHAPTER SIX

The Magic Genie Within Your Subconscious Mind

In Aladdin's Lamp resided a Magic Genie, who would carry out any wish Aladdin had. All he had to do was rub the magic lamp and the Genie would appear ready to carry out his bidding.

Your subconscious mind might be likened to this Genie. It is ready to carry out any command that you give it. And like the Magic Genie, your subconscious mind is a powerful aid, a dynamic force that can be harnessed for great achievement.

When you see a great pianist like Vladimir Horowitz sit at the piano and play a difficult concerto with such ease and fluency, it is because he has spent years in building the habit patterns of perfection in his mind. The subconscious stores these memoires and releases them under automatic control, so the pianist need not consciously think of how he going to play the difficult score.

All your habit patterns can be built in your subconscious mind so they become automatic responses of your body functions. You can learn how to become a great speaker, writer, composer, musician, inventor, or business success. You may consciously choose the things you want your subconscious to do for you automatically, and then by constant repetition of the act or thought, you will imprint it on your subconscious mind, making it a part of the automatic reflex action of your subconscious.

Modern psychosomatic medicine has shown that one's mental attitude also has much to do with sickness or health. When you constantly repeat positive statements such as, "I am healthy. I am happy. I am young. I have vitality and energy," you actually help raise the energy levels of your body and release the stored sugar in your liver, giving you greater vitality.

The subconscious accepts as truth whatever you tell it often enough. When you repeat an idea over and over again, your subconscious mind automatically accepts it as gospel, and sets to work making it a reality in your life. In psychology, this is known as the Law of Predominant Mental Impression. It simply means that you must keep repeating an idea, saying it over so often that it becomes a law for your subconscious mind.

For instance, if you keep telling yourself, "I can't do that, I'm afraid I'll fail, I'm inferior and inadequate, I'm tired and weak, I'm afraid I'll catch cold," you will make these negative statements the laws of your subconscious mind. As this mind automatically carries out everything you think or say many times, the sympathetic nervous system will set these negative forces into motion. You will become more and more fearful. You will do things that make you fail. You will become inferior. You will be constantly tired and weak. You set the mental stage for the action you imprint upon the subconscious mind.

One of the best ways to reach your subconscious mind and imprint upon it the things you want it to do, is to begin to act the part you wish to play in life. If you want to be rich and successful, act as though you already are. If you want to be happy, begin to act as though you are already happy: smile, be optimistic, talk about the good things of life instead of the sad and evil things. Your subconscious reacts according to the emotional pattern that you set for yourself. If you act happy and successful, your subconscious will send positive pulsations to your glands and the entire rhythm of your body will change to a positive one.

When Napoleon decided he would become Emperor of France, he called in François-Joseph Talma, one of the nation's leading tragedians, to show him how to walk, talk, and look like an emperor. Napoleon had a real problem, for he was scarcely five feet tall. The actor made him strut back and forth, giving commands as an emperor would; he showed him how to stand, how to talk, how to think like an emperor. Finally, when Napoleon was ready to declare himself Emperor Napoleon the First, he carried such conviction that the crowed heads of Europe bowed before him.

If you act a part long enough, your subconscious mind will be impressed by it, and make it living reality. You can begin to achieve a strong, more dynamic personality by this art of impersonation. Stand before a mirror and speak to yourself. Tell yourself that you are strong, dynamic, good looking: really believe the things you are going to become. Then go around *being* the person you wish to be. Soon, it will become second nature. You will be guided to doing the things you have long acted out. People will begin to see you as the person you have mentally thought yourself to be.

Elsewhere we are told of the importance of writing down your desires and ambitions. Now it is time for you to know how this simple act works to imprint upon your subconscious mind the suggestions you write down. Your subconscious mind believes everything that is repeated to it often enough—things that are said or written down. The kinetic action of *doing* something with your hands more forcibly impresses the subconscious than if you just *think* a thing.

Another great secret for releasing subconscious power is to read or talk aloud. There is something magical about the hypnotic power of the human mind. When you give yourself autosuggestions, and believe what you are telling yourself, you are deeply imprinting the subconscious mind with what you say.

Review these facts for great subconscious power:

1. Turn over the automatic function of your body completely to your subconscious mind. Stop worrying about the way your body works and trust your subconscious to take care of it.

2. Use the system of autosuggestion devised by French mind theorist Emile Coué, and every night just before you drift off to sleep whisper to yourself at least twenty

times, "Every day in every way, I am getting better and better." Do the same immediately upon waking in the morning.

3. Memorize other autosuggestions which you repeat every day when you have a few minutes of time, such as, "I can do this job perfectly. I will win a promotion and a raise in salary. I like other people, and they like me. I can be a big success. I am bigger than I think." You can make up your own suggestions to fit your needs.

4. Write down your main dream or goal at least once a week, and keep where you can see it every day. Keep reviewing it in your mind until it becomes second nature.

5. Sit quietly for ten minutes a day and pass through your imagination mental pictures of yourself doing things you really want to do, such as singing, acting, being in your own business, living in a new house, buying a car, taking a long trip. The important thing is to keep reviewing the picture in detail, until it is such a big part of your consciousness that your subconscious will take it up and act on it.

CHAPTER SEVEN

Duplicate the Power of the Great Men of History

When Thomas Edison failed time after time in perfecting his electric light bulb he never stopped trying to find some substance that would last more than a few seconds in the filaments of his lamps. He was so resourceful that he tried thousands of different substances, and each time he failed. But still he did not give up. One day his assistant become so discouraged that he said, "Mr. Edison you've tried ten thousand times and failed, why don't you give up?"

Edison replied, "No, I can't give up. Now we know ten thousand things that won't work." And soon he found something that *did work*.

If you wish to be great and make your fortune, learn how to duplicate the power of the greatest men and women in history. These figures discovered The Million Dollar Secret, some by accident, others through inspiration or sheer dint of hard work and persistent effort.

There are three things that will make you outstanding in any business field, and these three things were present in the works of all geniuses:

1. Ability to know your own talents and possibilities.
2. Daring to attempt the seeming impossible.
3. Courage to persist in the face of obstacles.

The step of determining what you want, and letting your desires guide you to the path you wish to take, is the most important in applying the Million Dollar Secret to your own life and success.

Follow this step-by-step formula to greatness:

1. Pick the field you wish to specialize in; learn all you can about it, study the lives of its outstanding successes, then strive to emulate their pattern of thinking.
2. Each day strive to put into action one or more of the qualities or traits that you have learned from the lives of great men. Imitate these thoughts, if need be, at first, then you will gradually begin to originate great thoughts and actions of your own.
3. Get specialized training to perfect your gifts and talents. Assemble facts about the work you choose; see the good and bad sides, then, if you remain interested, let no one divert you from your goal.
4. Let what I call Divine Discontent motivate you in your desire to achieve perfection. Never be satisfied with your present accomplishments or progress. When you are satisfied, you cease to grow. Everything in nature is in constant flux, from an imperfect to a more perfect state. Constantly desire change and evolvement.

5. Aim for the stars, even though you may not achieve them; at least such an ambition will assure you of reaching some kind of high goal. Browning said, "Ah, but a man's reach should exceed his grasp, / Or what's a heaven for?"

6. Create a vortex of mental activity about yourself. Break the inertia that may be holding you back by doing *something*, almost anything is preferable to sitting back and refusing to make an effort.

7. Never be satisfied with the limitations that life seems to have placed on you and your expression of your talents. There are means and possibilities all about you— search them out and use them. Part of our Million Dollar Secret is the building of mental power, so you may better express your God-given gifts and talents.

Chapter Eight

The Million-Dollar Personality That Wins

S ome people seem to be born lucky. They grow up in circumstances that seem favorable for their maturing into well-balanced, integrated personalities. They seem to possess charm and attractiveness; everyone seems to like them, and want to help them.

Others are less fortunate. They are born in environments that may be negative and shabby, surrounded by people who are negative, fearful, financially pinched, and constantly worried. These people acquire mental habits that are difficult to break in adult life.

Epictetus said of habit: "Every habit and faculty is preserved and increased by correspondent actions, as the habit of walking, by walking, or running, by running."

The more you practice thinking or doing a thing, the easier it becomes, until finally, by building positive mental habits you are able to perform consistently at a high level of action in the expression of your personality.

It is possible for you now to choose the type of persona you want to be, just as you choose the suit or dress you want to wear. Psychologists tell us that we are conditioned by our own minds through suggestions and opinions we hold, or tell ourselves. If you constantly tell yourself you are inferior, you will gradually begin to take on the hang-dog appearance of an inferior person. You will shrink from contact with people. They will sense your reactions and shy away from you.

If you make it a point to reinforce your ego by telling yourself you are worthy of the best life has to offer, and that you are likeable, pleasant, happy, and loving towards others, people will instantly feel your power and gravitate toward you.

Building a magnetic personality is easy when you once know how. It is a matter of satisfaction to be able to win friends and hold them, but it has intrinsic value also that can be counted in actual dollars and cents. Tests given by psychologists proved that men and women who had studied their personalities and worked to perfect and polish them actually got more jobs as executives than those who had inferior personalities but great ability. If it comes to a choice between a pleasant, cheerful, happy-appearing person for a job, and one who is morose and sullen all the time, ability being equal, the pleasant person will be selected every time.

CHAPTER NINE

Ten Steps That Can Make You a Mental Giant

B efore you begin your study of this part of the Million Dollar Secret, I ask that you rid your mind of all doubts and uncertainties, and do *really believe you can do the things I am going to tell you about.* Remove the shadows of fear and doubt and limitation that may fill your mind, and then become imbued with only one thought: *you can do anything you desire!*

Make these ten steps part of your life:

1. **Listen to the Master Mind within.** There is a vast intelligence in all of nature that regulates and operates the entire universe. This Master Mind also works through your own mind; if you learn how tap its power you will have increased your mental capacity at least fifty percent. See how this Master Mind works in nature. The maple tree produces seed that the Master Mind has given wings, like a parachute. Why wings? Because this Intelligence *knows* that if maple seeds fall in the shade of the mother tree they will have little chance to survive, so they have wings that the wind can catch and blow to a sunny patch of ground. This Intelligence leaves nothing to chance to assure the suc-

cess and perpetuity of her creation; she gives the maple tree literally thousands of winged seed, to be sure that some of them will survive the caprices of Fate. Learn to listen to the Master Mind within. Be in tune with it; it wants your success and happiness *more than you do!*

2. **Expand your thinking to encompass broader fields of experience and action.** Most people limit themselves to habit-patterns of thought that include their small, everyday happenings. They never allow themselves to soar into the unlimited world of creative thought where they envision wonderful experiences, better jobs, bigger income, the accumulation of a fortune. The habit patterns of thought become chains that bind them to lives of inactivity, poverty, and limitation. Learn to *think big!* Your brain cells are aching for exercise in big thinking. Consider the limitations of thought in those people you know. Most of them are in positions where they make a limited income and they are doing nothing to change their mode of thought or life. Samuel Johnson said: "The true, strong, and sound mind is the mind that can embrace equally great things and small."

3. **Gather as much knowledge as you can consciously— then let your subconscious take over.** Most people make too much effort to do the really big things of life. They seem to feel, somehow, that they have to do the actual work. Stop and ask yourself what power it is within you that does your breathing, that digests your

food, that works your mind. You will then realize that the really big things are done for you by your subconscious. To let your subconscious work better for you, gather as much knowledge as you can consciously about the subjects you wish to become expert in, then turn over this mass of material to your subconscious and let it do the work of sorting out, storing, filing, and using the knowledge you have accumulated.

4. **Give yourself a five-year plan for mental growth.** Your mind likes *definiteness*. Give yourself a five-year plan for study, growth, and evolvement. In that time promise yourself a completely new mental viewpoint, new environment, new work, new friends, a higher income, and better standards of living. Your mind likes such a challenge as this. It will rise to the occasion and give you the mental power you may need to achieve your five-year goal. Do not stop, however, with a five-year plan; keep expanding and changing this plan as the years go on, so that you always have an unfinished symphony of life which you are working to complete. This gives added purposefulness to living. Pick the books you want to study in that five-year plan, the courses you wish to take, the steps you wish to use to set up a new social life, the friends you wish to cultivate. *Do more than just think about these things*; write them down, make a comprehensive list of your plans and aspirations, so you can consult your list frequently and see that you are on the right path.

5. **Create a need in your life for something you want.** Do not vaguely say, "I want more money," "I'd like to visit Europe next year," or "I'd like to get married." These kinds of statements are weak and inconclusive. Everyone thinks such thoughts once in a while. You must create a need in your life for the things you want. If you want more money, *find a need for more money.* What do you want more money for? Be specific and tell yourself what you will do with it. Why do you want to go to Europe? For fun? For cultural improvement? To meet a rich marriage partner? For relaxation and rest? Have a real need, and keep reaffirming that need, until it crystallizes in your mind as a dynamic demand on the universal life intelligence.

6. **Make your mind do some creative act each day.** Nothing builds latent mental powers so much as each day making your mind do some creative act. You may not see any immediate results in these small creative efforts but you can take my word for it, they will gradually build giant mental power. Victor Herbert wrote music for more than forty years *without winning recognition*, but every day he sat down and courted the creative muse within, writing a little, patiently waiting and perfecting his talents. Forty years later he won his great success with *Babes in Toyland*, and established himself for all time in the light opera and musical comedy field.

7. **When you experience defeats come back and try again.** A muscle grows by repeated exercise; a brain cell

grows *only* when you keep trying, thinking, studying to develop your mind. You need persistent and daily mental exercise if you wish to build your mental power to its fullest capacity. Increase your mental capacity by repeating your efforts over and over, even in the face of seeming defeats. When someone asked the mighty Babe Ruth what he thought about when he stood on the diamond waiting for the pitcher to throw the ball, the great Babe replied, "I think of only one thing; of hitting the ball!" Your mind must have this persistent and determined feeling about the goal you are trying to achieve.

8. **Accept no limitation on your mental powers.** This priceless ingredient of our Million Dollar Secret is vitally important. Many times it is not the knowledge, the talent, the greatness that a person possesses that brings him success, fame, and fortune. A little talent will go a long way if a person refuses to accept limitations on his abilities.

9. **Organize your thinking by organizing your life.** Order and harmony are God's first laws for creation. If you live in a constant state of confusion and disorder, you cannot have an orderly mind. You can begin today to organize your thinking. You start by first organizing your life. Have a daily schedule and organized surroundings. This will help you acquire the habit of neat and orderly thinking, and your mind will soon release

power to do these things in an easier manner than if left to haphazard chance.

10. **Be inspired by noble emotions and high ideals.** No person has ever achieved great heights who was not first inspired by noble emotions and high ideals. Absorb great works of art, writing, and music—read inspiring biographies and emulate their examples. Create beauty and greatness.

CHAPTER TEN

Become a Receiving Station for Great Ideas

There is a saying in philosophy, "As above, so below." This means that the microcosm, man, reflects all the processes and creative principles that exist in the macrocosm, or the larger universe. Microcosm relates to an organism, regarded as a world in miniature. Man is actually a world in miniature, and he reflects in all his mental and physical processes, all the universal processes of growth, attraction, reproduction, and refinement. The seedling of reality is in man's own mind; his mind is where he creates the world in which he lives.

Once you understand this principle, you will know that part of the Million Dollar Secret lies hidden in your mind as the creative power that every person has locked within his own human consciousness.

There is a picture or pattern within your mind, which has its counterpart in Universal Intelligence—the same intelligence that creates the rose and the oak tree. There is only one major difference between use of this Creative Power within your mind and that in nature: You, being a creature of volition and choice, *may choose the pictures you wish to create in the outer world*, whereas animals, birds, insects, and growing organisms in nature are *forced to create according to a set pattern.*

What one man has thought, experienced, or done may be the common property of all creative minds. You can reflect the knowledge of all the great minds since the beginning of time. Just as all chicks within the hen's egg know how to peck their way out of the shell, so too, your Creative Intelligence knows how to work out all your problems, knows how to give you the ideas and inspiration to make your dreams come true.

You can become a receiving station for great ideas, just as the famous men of history did. You can unlock the creative power of this higher mind within you, just as Napoleon did, as Michelangelo did in his creative masterpieces of marble and canvas. The power that was used by Lincoln, Columbus, Newton, Edison, Washington, and Benjamin Franklin is a part of your own higher consciousness. You may tap the creative mind within and receive from it all the inspiration you need to build your future destiny in the pattern of greatness and genius.

Here is how to use this method to become a receiving station for great ideas:

1. Each night before going to bed spend a few moments picturing in your mind's eye the things you want to achieve, the things you wish to attract, the qualities and talents you want for your own, and even the people you want in your life. Feel that these things are already in existence awaiting your joyous discovery.

2. Ask the "Father Within" to point the way to right work, to the finding or making of the money you need to pay your debts; to the knowledge you need to get a better salary; to the finding of lost or hidden objects. The great ESP researcher Dr. J.B. Rhine tells in his book *Extra-Sensory Perception* of how a girl, whose father had died, needed money desperately. She dreamed one night that her father came to her and told her to look in the secret compartment of an antique dresser. She found it, and stuffed in there were many big bills. How was this knowledge conveyed? Telepathy? Spiritualism? Vibration? Science does not yet know, but there is something at work in another dimension of the universe, which seems to represent a higher mind. Put your problems to this higher mind within, ask for a solution, and then quietly go to sleep confident that the answer will come to you, either in a dream or when you awaken.

3. If you wish to pick up thoughts of greatness, such as those that inspired the geniuses of the past, sit quietly in your room alone, and meditate on the great person whose imagination you wish to contact. If it is Beethoven, hold his name in your mind; acquire as much knowledge as you can of his life; be conversant with his great music; then sit and wait for the highest inspiration to come through to you. Do the same with any great figure: a scientist, inventor, or business success.

4. You can convey messages to others through this process of speaking to the higher mind within you. Tell the higher mind what you want to convey; hold the name and face of the person in mind; then talk to them as you would if they were there in person. You can also receive mental messages from others through this same process of concentration and visualization. Hold in mind the face of the person you wish to receive messages from; concentrate your mind on that person for a while, and then sit perfectly still and wait and see what thoughts come into your mind.

Chapter Eleven

How to Seek and Win the Aid of Important People

You've heard the saying, "Nothing succeeds like success." Also, "Money seeks out money." It is true, if you wish to win fame and fortune, you can seldom do it on your own. You must seek out the aid of wealthy and important people.

The Quaker father advised his daughter, "Marry thee not for money, but go thee where money is."

The working of the law of proximity is influential in the lives of many people who have achieved success in their chosen profession. It isn't so much *what* they know as *whom* they know. This has become a cliché in American business, but is nevertheless true. Few of the great geniuses in history could have possibly succeeded without the aid of others.

Edison was a great inventor, but his inventions would have been worthless to the world if they *had not been marketed*. Ford had a great idea in building his horseless carriage, but he needed capital and backing before he could mass-produce his motorcar. Raphael and Michelangelo created great masterpieces in art but they needed their reigning princes of state and church, and the aid of influential, wealthy men and women to give them the means to achieve their great works of art.

It is said, "A man is known through the company he keeps." Most people achieve greatness through reflection. It is just as easy in life to choose the company of friends who are important, politically powerful, creatively active, and wealthy, as to associate with people who are shabby, disorderly in their thinking, lazy, disreputable, shiftless, and negative.

It is important, in building your future career, to choose friends who are striving for the same goals as you; or people who *have already achieved these goals*. It is just as easy to form friendships with people who are going places as to select those who are doomed by their negative habits to failure.

"Hitch your wagon to a star" is a saying that applies to the forming of friendships. Everyone you admit into your life on a close, personal basis should measure up to certain standards. Ask yourself:

- Will our friendship by mutually good?
- What have I to offer this person, and what has he to give?
- Does he have habits that are negative and that might impede my course in life?
- Are his standards high?
- Have I anything to learn from my association with this friend?

It is not selfish for you to be concerned about these new associations, for if you see a person more than three times, he has the power to change your life. You want to be sure that, given such tremendous power, these new friends will change your life for the better.

So many people plan every detail of their lives carefully, and yet completely ignore their social lives. More business is done over cocktails and on golf courses than in offices. It is true that very often, important, busy executives snatch these opportunities of relaxation and conviviality to discuss business matters and make important decisions. Take advantage of this psychological fact. It is easier after a businessman has had a few drinks and eaten a good meal to get his attention than it is to go to his office and get through a retinue of assistants and secretaries.

I recall two meetings with noted authors that came about in such relaxed surroundings in my own career. One was the great humorist, Irvin Cobb, who was a guest of honor at a luncheon I attended. The other was Rupert Hughes, a great American writer, who I met at a party. Because he was slightly deaf and wore a hearing aid, many people found it difficult to talk to the noted author. I made it a special point to speak distinctly and loudly when addressing him, keeping my face turned towards him so he could read my lips. I spent an instructive and pleasant hour in his company, and when the evening was over, he invited me to lunch, and at another time to play golf with him at the Lakeside Country Club near Hollywood. At the club that day alone, Mr. Hughes introduced me to some of the biggest directors, producers, and stars who later helped my career immeasurably. I was then in my early twenties, and *such contacts would have been impossible without the aid of a well-known and important person.*

Use these secrets for winning the aid of important people:

1. Offer your services and aid to civic betterment groups in your community. Here you will meet people who are in key positions and who can help you immeasurably in achieving your goal.

2. Become affiliated with your local political groups, for they have prestige and power. Many a man has started as a lowly assistant in a political ward, and risen to a position of power and prominence. You can meet lawyers, judges, and those who are big in politics, and through their aid and influence you can be selected to big-paying jobs.

3. Join a veteran's group, or the American Legion, if you qualify, or any other group that is active in your community. Not only does this pave the way to social activity, but it can lead to an expansion of your business contacts and a position of prestige.

4. Get in the habit of writing to important people, suggesting ideas for the betterment of the community, or offering your help in some charitable work being undertaken. Occasionally write a letter praising the official, and he will definitely take note of you. I have

known people who got in to see the heads of some of the biggest businesses in the country through this practice.

5. Use your vacation time profitably. Plan your vacation so that you come in contact with people who might prove valuable to your career.

6. Do not be afraid to present your ideas to important business executives or wealthy people. They are constantly searching for new ideas, new talent, new markets. If you bring them an idea that changes their business for the better, you may work yourself right into an important position. I know one young man who sent a suggestion to the Canadian Pacific Railroad president for ways of increasing tourist riders, and the president instantly arranged an interview that led the young man to lucrative post.

7. In making contacts with important people, show interest in them and their work. Have respect for their advice and opinions. They have risen in their profession because of specialized skills; respect their judgment.

8. Build the other person's ego, for if he *is* important he will appreciate recognition of that fact. Even great people have their low moments.

9. When you meet people who are important and who might prove helpful, find a common ground of interest, which you can use as a basis for a friendship. This might be work you have in common, school friends you both know, a sport that you can share, and so on.

10. Try to discuss things that are pleasant and noncontroversial. Avoid politics and religion. You are judged by the things you talk about.

11. Package your personality so it shows your best side. This means you should have a pleasant, affable, and relaxed personality, one that is easy to get along with. Practice smiling, and learn how to have a good, hearty laugh, for a good laugh is infectious and often helps win friends. Everyone wants to laugh; no one really wants to share your sad experiences and cry.

12. Give freely of yourself, if you wish to attract and hold the interest of important people. If you have nothing else of value to give the world, give yourself, your interest, your enthusiasm, your charm, your attention, your consideration, and, *most important of all*, your sincere friendship.

CHAPTER TWELVE

Take These Seven Steps Up the Ladder of Success

There is a formula for success that is as definite as the laws that govern mathematics. Success consists of several different component parts, and these are as absolute as the law of gravity.

STEP 1. THE DESIRE TO ACHIEVE

We have spoken elsewhere of desire, but in connection with achieving success, it is vitally important that you use this Emotion of Desire correctly. Everyone wants to succeed. Everyone wants fame and fortune. What you must do is *define exactly the type of success you desire.* The concrete image must exist in your mind first. It is the pattern by which Universal Intelligence can cut the cloth to make the suit you have chosen.

STEP 2. YOUR DREAM OR INNER VISION

All outward forms of creation in the world began with a dream or inner vision. Everyone has some kind of dream of the world in which he wishes to live. This dream resides in the mind, and is instilled by our early childhood thoughts and experiences. You played house, and expressed the idea of love and marriage and having your own family some day. You played doctor and had the dream of someday being one in real life. Dreams crystalize into reality when you apply this formula correctly. It has been said that an idea, when it comes with the force of revelation, will lead to a revolution in your life. The overpowering *idea you hold in your mind* about the life you wish to lead is *the dream or inner vision* that will shape your entire future. You must have this dream firmly fixed and never stray from it.

STEP 3. RELEASE CREATIVE IMAGINATION

Literally, imagination means the act or power of forming mental images of what is not present. It is also the act or power of creating new ideas by combining previous experiences. Creative Intelligence carries you a step further, however, than just forming mental images; it means to cause to come into existence, to make or originate, to cause, to produce, to bring about. When you creatively imagine something you are actually causing it to come into being, for you are *forming it first in your own mind*.

STEP 4. THE POWER OF CONCENTRATION

A lightening bolt can split a giant oak tree because of its concentrated power. The power of concentration is terrific when released in your mind. Most people scatter their mental energy and force by spending ninety percent of their time in thinking over past defeats and disappointments. Their minds spend hours dwelling on the negative aspects of their lives: the failures, the tragedies, the sicknesses, the lost investments. This tendency to concentrate on the negative aspects of life only helps to inscribe these things deeper into the workings of the brain. In using the positive power of concentration, learn to reverse your failures, not to rehearse them, which only tends to make them more real in your mind.

STEP 5. THE POWER OF INTUITION

The humming bird needs no instructor in the art of constructing his thistle-down-lined, swinging nest. Something within him *knows how to construct it perfectly!* The ant requires no one to tell him how to organize his nest and build an anthill. This is an intuitive function within his mind. Emerson spoke of this Intuitive Mind Within in these brilliant words:

> *A man should learn to detect and watch that gleam of light which flashes across his mind from within, more than the lustre of the firmament of bards and sages. Yet, he dismisses without notice his thought, because it is his. In every work of genius we recognize our own rejected thoughts; they come back to us with a certain alienated majesty. Trust thyself; every heart vibrates to that iron string.*

STEP 6. HABIT PATTERNS OF SUCCESS

Study the following questions carefully, for each is a key to the building of new habit patterns of success:

- Are you efficient?
- Are you punctual?
- Are you honest?
- Do you give full value?
- Are you positive?
- Are you confident?
- Are you thrifty?
- Do you know how to handle money?
- Are you able to organize people?
- Are you outgoing in your personality?
- Are you orderly, clean, neat?
- Do you recognize big ideas?
- Do you persist in the face of obstacles?
- Do you believe in yourself?
- Do you think and talk only success?

STEP 7. FAITH IN YOUR DESTINY

Faith in yourself and faith in your destiny—this is an essential step in your climb up the ladder of success. Many talented people never make it because they do not possess this essential ingredient of the Million Dollar Secret.

The twentieth-century novelist Howard Fast wrote a book some years ago. He sent it out to several publishers. They all turned it down. No one had faith in it. Fast had such faith in the ultimate success of the book that he raised

$1,000 and published it himself. Only a few hundred copies existed, and undoubtedly, for a time, for a very small sum, anyone could have bought the movie rights.

Then one day a producer read the book, and offered Fast a large sum for the movie rights. *Spartacus* was the name of the book that Howard Fast had faith in. It became one of the great motion pictures of its time, and also smashed the infamous Hollywood blacklist.

Faith in yourself is the "open sesame" to riches and fame. It matters not that others lack faith in you or your works; if you really believe in yourself and your talents, you will build inspiration and power to persist until you have achieved your life goal.

"All things are possible to him that believeth."

About the Author

Born in 1908 in Upstate New York, ANTHONY NORVELL was a popular writer on occult and esoteric topics, particularly the uses of visualization and mind metaphysics. He lectured widely on both coasts, including weekly talks at New York's Carnegie Hall. *The Million Dollar Secret Hidden in Your Mind*, originally published in 1963, is his most popular and enduring book. He died in 1990.

About Mitch Horowitz

MITCH HOROWITZ is the PEN Award-winning author of books including *Occult America* and *The Miracle Club*. A writer-in-residence at the New York Public Library and lecturer-in-residence at the University of Philosophical Research in Los Angeles, Mitch introduces and edits G&D Media's line of Condensed Classics and is the author of the Napoleon Hill Success Course series, including *The Miracle of a Definite Chief Aim*, *The Power of the Master Mind*, and *Secrets of Self-Mastery*. He is on Twitter @MitchHorowitz and on Instagram @MitchHorowitz23.

9 781722 505172